Science Experiments You Can Eat

VICKI COBB

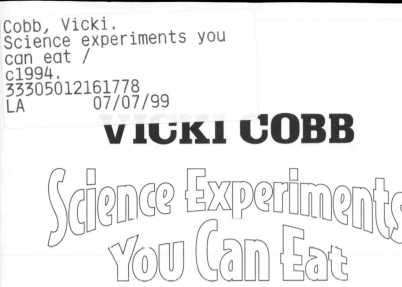

Science Experiments You Can Eat

REVISED AND UPDATED

illustrated by David Cain

HarperCollins*Publishers*

Acknowledgments

The author extends heartfelt thanks to the following people but accepts full responsibility for the accuracy of the text: Louise Slade, Ph.D., G. Curtis Busk, Ph.D., and Caroline Fee of Nabisco Biscuit Company; Dr. Jeffrey Stamp of Frito-Lay; Duane MacDonald of General Mills; and Dr. Ann Hollingsworth of Bil Mar Foods.

Library of Congress Cataloging-in-Publication Data
Cobb, Vicki.
    Science experiments you can eat / Vicki Cobb ; illustrated by David Cain. — Revised and updated.
        p.   cm.
    Includes index.
    Summary: Experiments with food demonstrate various scientific principles and produce an eatable result. Includes rock candy, grape jelly, cupcakes, and popcorn.
    ISBN 0-06-023534-9. — ISBN 0-06-023551-9 (lib. bdg.)
    1. Science—Experiments—Juvenile literature.   2. Cookery—Juvenile literature.
[1. Science—Experiments. 2. Experiments. 3. Cookery.] I. Cain, David, date, ill. II. Title.
Q164.C52   1994   93-13679
507.8—dc20   CIP
                                                                 AC

Typography by Elynn Cohen
5 6 7 8 9 10
❖
Revised Edition

To the memory of Paula Wolf, my mother,
for whom cooking was an act of love

Contents

Science Experiments
You Can Eat

Food for Thought

Think about food often? Who doesn't? Imagine a hot fudge sundae, how it smells and looks and tastes. Are the juices flowing in your mouth yet? Thoughts of food can do that. You probably think about food at least ten times a day—whenever your stomach growls, or you read a menu, or pass a bakery, or smell a deli, or follow a recipe, or plan a party, or go to the supermarket.

When my two sons were growing up, planning meals and shopping for food were part of my job. I experimented with recipes to make the job interesting for myself. One day a friend called and suggested that we collaborate on writing a cookbook

for kids. I said, "Let me think about it." I hung up the phone and walked to the window. As I looked out over the Hudson River, I thought, "I don't want to write a cookbook for kids. I want to write science books for kids." The words "science experiments you can eat" popped into my head. Suddenly I had a whole new way to think about food. One that opened up countless possibilities for experimenting in the kitchen. The book was published in 1972 and has new readers every year.

But a lot has happened since then. Microwave ovens are now popular. New fruits and vegetables have come onto the market. A few items have disappeared from supermarket shelves. I've kept on learning. It was time for me to take another look at experimenting with food.

So here is an updated version of *Science Experiments You Can Eat*. It has all of the old experiments plus lots of new ones. The purpose of this book remains the same: to use food and cooking to learn about science.

If you're not hungry to learn about science, this book will whet your appetite. It is designed to nourish your curiosity and feed your mind. The ideas in this book are as easy to digest as the food. In a way, it's like a cookbook. You can use it to prepare many different dishes, although you might

change your mind about eating them when you get your results. (I've done every experiment, but I must confess that I haven't eaten every experiment.) This book combines learning about science with eating—two of life's greatest pleasures. And it gives you a legitimate reason to play with your food.

EXPERIMENTING WITH FOOD

Next time you sit down to eat, try to figure out how all the things on your plate began. All foods were once alive or produced by a living thing. Sometimes the food on your table has no resemblance to the animals and plants from which it came.

Many changes in food take place before it reaches your home. Some foods are prepared from only a part of a living thing, such as wheat germ, lard, or sugar. Many foods are processed so they will keep longer without spoiling. Chemicals are often added to breads and cakes to keep them moist and to crackers and potato chips to keep them dry and crisp. Fruits, vegetables, and meats are canned, dried, or frozen to keep harmful bacteria from making them unfit to eat. But in some cases, the growth of bacteria or other microorganisms is necessary, such as in the preparation of bread, cheese, yogurt, and vinegar.

Cooking changes food still further. Heat makes some food softer and some food firmer. It changes the color of many foods. Different flavors blend when heated together. Heat destroys harmful bacteria and makes certain foods easier to digest.

It's easy to produce changes in food, and producing change is part of what science is about. If you can produce a change in a certain food, you can learn something about the properties of that food by studying the way it changes.

All of the experiments in this book are designed to show changes. Sometimes the changes are not obvious, and you have to look closely to see if one has even occurred. But when you know what you are looking for, even a small change can be very exciting. Every experiment has been tested, but the materials you use and the conditions in your kitchen may be slightly different from those described in this book. If you don't get the expected results, try to think of what factors might have caused the different results, and how you can redesign the procedure to produce the expected results.

HOW TO USE THIS BOOK

Be sure you know *what* you are doing in an experiment and *why* you are doing it. Every chapter has a

short introduction that discusses the subject you will be investigating. Every experiment also has a short introduction that asks a question you can answer by doing the experiment.

The materials and equipment needed are listed at the beginning of each experiment. Collect everything before you begin. This way you will not be caught without some important item at a critical time during the experiment.

The procedure section tells you how to do the experiment. Often, reasons for doing a certain step are discussed as you go along. Since timing is important, you should read and understand the whole procedure section before you start the experiment.

There are certain standard practices for safety and use of equipment in every laboratory, and your kitchen is no exception. Consult the cook in your house before you start experimenting and ask for help with any procedures you are not sure about.

After the procedure section there is a brief discussion of what your results mean. Often, you are directed in your observations by questions. I don't always tell you what your results should be. This gives you the opportunity to get answers for yourself from your experiments, just as real scientists do.

As you do these experiments, questions of your own will occur to you. You may get ideas for experiments of your own design. So do them! Don't

worry that you are getting sidetracked. Believe it or not, finding something interesting and getting side-tracked is the goal of every working scientist. Your own discoveries are what make science an adventure! This book is your road map. Bon voyage and bon appétit!

Solutions

The "stuff" that makes up food, you, and everything else in the universe is called *matter*. Chemists are scientists who study matter and how it changes. They define matter as anything that has weight and takes up space.

When scientists first tackled the study of matter, they had to deal with the problem that matter in its natural state is complicated. Very little matter in nature exists in a pure state. Most matter exists mixed up with other matter. A *solution*, such as seawater, is an especially interesting kind of mixture. One amazing thing about a solution is that it is evenly mixed or *homogeneous*. In a pail of seawater,

a cup taken from the top has exactly the same amount of salt in it as a cup taken from the bottom. Another amazing thing about solutions is that they become homogeneous *all by themselves*. No stirring is necessary.

Chemists have a way of thinking—a model—about solutions that accounts for their interesting properties. They say that solutions, like all matter, are made up of tiny particles too small to see. These particles are arranged in two phases. One phase is called the *solvent*. Water is the most common solvent around. The solvent phase is *continuous*. This means that the water particles are in contact with one another. The other phase is called the *solute*. Salt is a solute in seawater. The solute phase is *discontinuous*. Solute particles may occasionally bump into each other but for the most part they are surrounded by solvent particles. Salt water is a simple solution with one solvent and one solute. But seawater has a number of solutes. A solution may be made of one or more solvents and one or more solutes.

When a solute dissolves, the solute particles move through the solvent in a process called *diffusion*. You don't even have to stir. See for yourself. Drop a lump of sugar (a solute) into a glass of water (a solvent) and let it stand for a while. What hap-

pens to the lump of sugar? When you can no longer see any sugar crystals, taste the top of the solution with a straw. How can you tell that the sugar is present? Use the straw to taste the solution near the bottom of the glass. To do this, cover the top end of the straw with your finger before you lower the other end into the solution. When the bottom of the straw is where you want to take your sample, carefully move your finger to let a small amount of the solution rise in the straw. Keep your finger on the top of the straw as you raise the bottom end of the straw to your mouth. Lift your finger to let the solution run into your mouth. With this technique you can taste samples from all parts of the solution. But be careful to keep the disturbance to the solution as little as possible when you insert the straw. Is the solution

homogeneous? If it isn't, wait a while and taste again.

Solutions are important in the study of matter. You can often discover what a substance is by the solvent it dissolves in and by how much of it dissolves. Many chemical reactions take place in solution that will not take place in air. The experiments in this chapter will introduce you to some different solutions and some of the ways solutions are used to learn about matter.

ROCK CANDY:
RECOVERING SOLUTE CRYSTALS

It's easy to recover a solute if you don't care about keeping the solvent. Leave a water solution open to the air and the solvent will evaporate, leaving the solute behind. To recover the solute from all kinds of beverages, put small amounts in shallow dishes. The water evaporates from the large surface area.

Some solutes form *crystals* as the solvent evaporates. Crystals are solids that have a regular geometric shape, with many sides or faces. Take a close look at sugar and salt crystals with a magnifying lens. They have very different shapes.

Rock candy is simply very large sugar crystals. Grow some in the next experiment.

Materials & Equipment

+ ½ cup water
+ 1 cup sugar
+ a measuring cup
+ a small saucepan
+ a wooden spoon

+ 3 or 4 small shallow dishes (aluminum foil dishes work well)
+ a magnifying glass

Procedure

1 Pour the water into the saucepan. Measure out a cup of sugar. Put just a spoonful of this sugar in the water and stir. Use a wooden spoon to stir; it won't get hot the way a metal spoon would when you heat this solution later. Continue to add sugar by spoonfuls, stirring after each addition until the sugar dissolves. How many spoonfuls before the sugar stops dissolving no matter how much you stir? When this happens the solution is called a *saturated solution*.

2 Set the saucepan on low heat for a few minutes. What happens to the undissolved crystals as the solution gets warmer?

3 Turn off the heat and remove the saucepan from the stove. Add sugar again, spoonful by spoonful. How many spoonfuls do you need to make a saturated solution in hot water?

4 Pour all the remaining sugar from the measuring cup into the pan. Put the saucepan on the stove again and continue heating gently until all the sugar is dissolved. Then bring it to the boiling point and boil for about a minute. The solution should be thick and clear and contain no sugar crystals. Pour the solution into the small dishes while it is hot. It's not important to distribute the solution evenly.

Observations

Watch the solution as it cools. Be careful not to jolt it or disturb it in any way. Does the solution remain clear? If it becomes cloudy, take a close look at it with a magnifying glass. A clear solution that contains more solute than would normally dissolve at that temperature is said to be *supersaturated*. Supersaturated solutions are very unstable and the slightest disturbance will cause crystals to form, removing them from the solution.

Some candy, like fudge, depends on the forma-

tion of millions of tiny crystals. When you beat fudge, tiny crystals form quickly from a supersaturated solution.

If you don't beat fudge hard enough, the crystals will be larger and the fudge will feel grainy in your mouth.

To make rock candy, you want large crystals to grow, and this takes time, sometimes weeks. Let the solution stand undisturbed at room temperature for a week or more. Every day, carefully break off the crust of crystals that forms at the surface so that the water can continue to evaporate.

Rock candy crystals will form around any small object you put in the solution. Make rock candy lollipops by putting a swizzle stick in a glass of supersaturated sugar solution. They will also quickly form around a crystal of sugar dropped into the solution. Such a crystal is called a *seed crystal*. You might want to try using a colored crystal sprinkle as a seed crystal in a supersaturated solution.

The formation of crystals is one way chemists know when they've got pure matter, either an element or a compound. Crystals are also a clue to the structure of a substance. Scientists figure that the perfect shape of crystals is not an accident but is the result of a regular arrangement of the smallest particles of a substance. These particles, *atoms* and *molecules*, have a size (although it's way too small to see even with the strongest microscope) and a shape. The arrangement of the atoms or molecules of a crystal produces the shape of the crystal much as closely stacked bricks can produce only a rectangular stack.

Compare the shape of the rock candy crystals to the crystals of granulated sugar with a magnifying glass. Are they the same shape? Do sugar crystals have the same shape as salt crystals? Would you expect sugar molecules to have the same shape as salt molecules?

ICE POPS AND THE FREEZING POINT OF SOLUTIONS

One question that comes up over and over again in the laboratory is: How do you know when you have a pure substance? One way to answer this question is to see how a substance you know to be pure (usually because a manufacturer says so on the

label) behaves differently from a substance you know to be a mixture (because you made it yourself). It is well established that pure water freezes at 32° Fahrenheit or 0° Celsius. Does a solution freeze at the same temperature as pure water? Do the next experiment and find out.

Materials & Equipment

- ✦ 1 cup of a clear, not cloudy, canned or bottled fruit juice (cherry or grape or apple works well)
- ✦ water
- ✦ 6 5-ounce paper cups
- ✦ a pen

- ✦ 6 circles of cardboard big enough to cover the cups
- ✦ 6 swizzle sticks or wooden sticks
- ✦ 2 measuring cups (each cup should hold at least 1 liquid cup)

Procedure

When you set up this experiment you will put different amounts of fruit juice in each cup in a systematic way and then freeze all the cups. The first ice pop will be undiluted fruit juice as it comes from the can, the second will be ½ fruit juice and ½ water, the third will be ¼ fruit juice and ¾ water, and

so on. This systematic changing of the amount of water in a solution is called *serial dilution*. Laboratories in many industries use serial dilutions to test the strength of a substance to find out, for example, how much detergent to put in a washing machine or how much aspirin to take when you are sick.

Since the freezing point of the ice pops is to be compared to the freezing point of pure water, you will also make an ice pop that is pure water, without juice. This ice pop is called the *control*. A control is treated just like every other part of an experiment but does not contain the thing being tested so it can be used as a basis for comparison.

1 Start by marking the cups: Juice, $\frac{1}{2}$, $\frac{1}{4}$, $\frac{1}{8}$, $\frac{1}{16}$, and control.

The purpose of the cardboard circle covers is to hold each stick upright until the ice pop has frozen. The covers should be large enough to cover the tops of the cups without falling in. Punch a hole just large enough to insert a stick in the center of each cardboard circle. Place a stick in each hole.

2 Measure $\frac{1}{2}$ cup of water and pour it into the cup marked "control."

Measure out 1 cup of juice. Pour $\frac{1}{2}$ cup of this juice into a second measuring cup. Then pour re-

maining $\frac{1}{2}$ cup of juice into the
paper cup labeled "juice."

Add $\frac{1}{2}$ cup of water
to the second measuring
cup to bring the volume
up to 1 cup. Mix well.
Use the first measuring
cup to get $\frac{1}{2}$ cup of
this dilution. Pour
this into the paper
cup marked "$\frac{1}{2}$."

Add $\frac{1}{2}$ cup of water to the first dilution to again
bring the volume up to 1 cup. Mix well and use $\frac{1}{2}$
cup of this dilution to make the next ice pop in the
cup labeled "$\frac{1}{4}$."

Follow the same procedure to make ice pops
that are $\frac{1}{8}$ juice and $\frac{1}{16}$ juice.

3 Put the covers and sticks on each cup. Adjust
the sticks so that they just touch the bottoms
of the cups.

4 Put all six cups in your freezer. It is important
to place them at the same depth so they will
all be at the same temperature. After about 40 minutes, check to see how freezing is progressing by
jiggling each stick back and forth. As freezing occurs, you can feel the ice forming. Keep checking
about every 20 minutes. Which pop freezes first?

Which ice pop takes longest to freeze? Does it require more or less time to freeze a solution?

Observations

On the basis of your experiment, why is salt put on sidewalks in winter? Why is alcohol put in car radiators before the cold weather sets in? How can the temperature at which a solution freezes be used to tell how pure a substance is? Handbooks for chemists always list the freezing points of pure solvents. If they test the freezing point of a liquid in their lab and they don't get the freezing point they expect, they know that other substances must be present.

When the ice pops are frozen solid, which may take several hours, your experiment is completed and you may eat them. Although some of the ice pops will taste better than others, even the control can be refreshing on a hot day. Just tear off the paper cup and enjoy!

FRUIT DRINKS
AND DISSOLVING RATES

Ever notice how some solutes dissolve faster than others? Can you think of some of the variables that

cause some solutions to form faster than others? In the next experiment see how temperature affects the rate at which a solute goes into a solvent.

Materials & Equipment

+ ½ cup ice water
+ ½ cup room-temperature water
+ ½ cup boiling water
+ I package of unsweetened Kool-Aid

+ sugar
+ 6½ cups cold water
+ a measuring cup
+ 3 clear glass tumblers
+ a 2-quart pitcher

Procedure

1 Put ½ cup of ice water in the first glass, ½ cup of water at room temperature in the second glass, and ½ cup of boiling water in the third glass.

2 Drop a small pinch of Kool-Aid into each glass. Watch how the Kool-Aid diffuses into solution.

Observations

In which glass does it dissolve most quickly? How long does it take for the Kool-Aid to diffuse evenly through the water?

Try this with other colored solutes like instant coffee or food coloring.

After you have finished the experiment, you can prepare the Kool-Aid to drink. Pour all the solutions into a 2-quart pitcher. Add the remaining Kool-Aid and the amount of sugar suggested on the package. Add $6\frac{1}{2}$ cups of cold water to bring the volume up to 2 quarts.

SOUR-BALL ADE

How does the amount of surface area of a solute affect the rate at which it dissolves in a solvent? The next experiment explores this idea.

Materials & Equipment

+ $\frac{3}{4}$ cup water, room temperature
+ 3 pieces of dark-colored hard candy (grape or cherry)

+ 3 small glasses
+ a measuring cup
+ waxed paper
+ a hammer or rolling pin

Procedure

1 Put $\frac{1}{4}$ cup of water into each glass.

2 Wrap one candy in waxed paper and tap it lightly with the hammer or rolling pin so it

breaks into several large pieces. Wrap another candy in waxed paper and smash it so it is like granulated sugar.

3 Drop the whole candy into the first glass, the broken candy into the second glass, and the smashed candy into the third glass.

Observations

Which candy has the most surface area? Which candy dissolves first? How do you think the amount of surface area affects the rate at which a solute dissolves? How do your findings explain why superfine sugar is used to sweeten iced drinks?

You can make a refreshing drink from this experiment. Pour all 3 solutions into one glass and add a few ice cubes. An orange slice adds a festive touch.

RED-CABBAGE INDICATOR

A sour taste is one indication of a type of solution called an *acid*. The word *acid* comes from a Latin word meaning sharp or biting to the taste. Acids also conduct electricity. A light bulb connected by wires to two electrodes will light up when the electrodes are submerged in an acid. Acids are not the only solutions that conduct electricity. Bases, also called *alkalies*, do the job as well.

Acids are present in many of the foods we eat. Lemon juice and vinegar are good examples. We also eat certain bases, although they are not as common as acids. Baking soda, for example, is a base when it is dissolved in water.

There are, of course, many stronger acids and bases that we don't eat because they are poisonous or extremely damaging to living tissues. Tasting is not a test used by chemists to determine whether or not a substance is an acid or a base. Instead, they use a dye called an *indicator* that changes color depending on what the solution is. Litmus paper turns blue when it is dipped in a base and pink when it is dipped in acid.

The pigment in red cabbage can be used as your own personal "litmus." Here's how to make some red-cabbage indicator.

Materials & Equipment

- 1 whole red cabbage
- water
- a knife
- a grater
- 2 large bowls
- measuring cups and spoons

- a slotted spoon
- a strainer
- a very clean glass jar and cover
- a small white dish

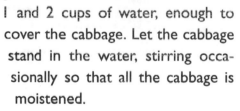

Procedure

1 Cut the cabbage into quarters. Grate it section by section into a large bowl. Add between 1 and 2 cups of water, enough to cover the cabbage. Let the cabbage stand in the water, stirring occasionally so that all the cabbage is moistened.

2 When the water is a strong red, remove as much of the grated cabbage as you can with the slotted spoon and save it in your second bowl. Pour the water solution through the strainer into the

glass jar. Add the strained cabbage to the rest of the cabbage you have saved.

3 Put about a tablespoon of your cabbage-juice indicator into a small white dish. Test for an acid by adding a substance you know to be an acid to the cabbage juice. Notice the color it becomes in acid. Now use a fresh sample of cabbage juice and add a substance you know to be a base (baking soda). Again notice the color change. Pretty gorgeous! Now add acid to the base-and-indicator mixture to reverse the color change. What happens when you add base to the indicator showing the acid color? An acid and a base will react with each other to neutralize each other. The original color of the red cabbage is pretty close to neutral. Now you can test some foods to see which category they fall into. Here is a list to get you started:

✦ Cooking water from boiled vegetables, including beans, peas, onions, carrots, turnips, celery, asparagus, etc.
✦ Liquids from canned vegetables and fruits
✦ Cream of tartar
✦ Soda pop
✦ Egg whites
✦ Fruit juices
✦ Tomatoes
✦ Cottage cheese

You can use the grated red cabbage raw in a salad or cole slaw, or you can experiment with it further.

Materials & Equipment

- ✦ shredded cabbage from above experiment
- ✦ 1 tart apple
- ✦ water
- ✦ a knife
- ✦ a wooden spoon

- ✦ 2 aluminum pots (The pot metal may be written on its underside. If you're not sure, ask the cook in your house.)

Procedure

1 Divide the cabbage evenly between the two aluminum pots. Cut the apple into quarters and remove the core. Cut the apple into chunks and add it to one of the pots. Add just enough water to cover the bottom of each pot ($\frac{1}{4}$–$\frac{1}{2}$ cup).

2 Then cook the cabbage over low heat for about 20 minutes, stirring occasionally.

Observations

Which cooked cabbage is redder? Which one contained acid? How do your findings support the idea that small amounts of aluminum combine with water to form aluminum hydroxide, a base? What did the apple do to this base?

You can also prepare your indicator from cooked cabbage but, of course, you can't cook it in an aluminum pot. Put raw grated cabbage in a stainless steel, porcelain, or glass pot and cover with water. Cook over low heat until it boils for 3 or 4 minutes. Then drain off your liquid. It will be a darker red than the uncooked indicator. Compare indicators to see which one you prefer using.

Mixed with salt, pepper, and butter, the cooked cabbage goes well with pot roast.

OPTICALLY ACTIVE SYRUPS

One characteristic of a true solution is that it is perfectly clear when you shine a light through it.

If you shine a special kind of light, called *polarized light,* through a syrup, you can see a pretty interesting property of some solutions. One way to create polarized light is to shine it through a lens of polarized sunglasses. It's hard to understand just what polarized light is because it involves three dimensions. Here's a way to think of it. Ordinary light is made up of waves, or beams. Imagine a single beam coming right at you. The beam would be a dot viewed from the end. Now imagine rays of light coming out of the beam at every possible angle. This should give you a mental image of how light travels in every direction. But when light strikes a polarized lens, only the rays traveling in one certain direction can pass through. The light that emerges from one polarized sunglass lens might be traveling in a vertical direction. If another lens Is put on top of the first and it is rotated so that it only allows light traveling in a horizontal direction to pass through, then the incoming light will be completely blocked. If you rotate one lens on top of the other, varying amounts of light will pass through.

Certain sugar solutions are *optically active*. This means that they have the ability to rotate polarized light. The next experiment is not a recipe but it shows pancake syrup in a new light.

Materials & Equipment

✦ various syrups in clear containers (maple, pancake, and corn syrups; diluted molasses; the sugar solution you made for rock candy)

✦ 2 lenses from a pair
of polarized sun-
glasses (make sure
you get permission
before you sacrifice
a pair of sunglasses
to science)

✦ a flashlight

Procedure

1 Line up the flashlight, one lens, a clear container with syrup, and the other lens as shown
in the picture. If the syrup doesn't come in a clear
bottle, pour it into a clear drinking glass.

2 Rotate the lens near your eye. An optically active syrup will produce a rainbow of colors,
one at a time as you turn the lens.

Observations

Polarized light (emerging from the first lens) that passes through the syrup is rotated from its entering position as it emerges from the syrup. Light contains waves of all different colors, but taken together they appear white. Even a beam of polarized light is made up of different waves. When light passes through the syrup, each colored wave is rotated by a slightly different amount. When you turn the second polarized lens in front of the syrup bottle, it filters out the separate waves so you see a sequence of colors through the second lens. The concepts of polarized light and optical activity are quite complicated, and you may want to read more about them in an optics book.

Biochemists use a device called a polarimeter to measure how optically active a sugar solution is. *Glucose*, one of the most important sugars we eat, is also called *dextrose* because it rotates polarized light to the right ("dextro" means "right"). *Fructose*, another kind of simple sugar, often found in fruit, is sometimes called *levulose*, because it rotates polarized light to the left. The optical activity of sugars is an important method in biochemistry for identifying sugars and understanding the structure of sugar molecules. The way a sugar solution acts in

polarized light is directly related to the structure of its molecules.

Unlike the syrup you made for rock candy, the syrups you buy for pancakes are designed to remain crystal free. Syrups that contain different kinds of sugars will not form crystals easily because the different sugar molecules don't fit together.

Suspensions, Colloids, and Emulsions

Matter is found in all kinds of mixtures, including mixtures with water. Figuring out all the different parts of mixtures is a challenge for scientists.

Water is called the universal solvent because more things dissolve in water than in any other liquid. But not everything dissolves in it. Some water mixtures, such as mud, contain particles that are heavy enough to settle on the bottom after being stirred up. This kind of mixture is called a *suspension*

because the material is suspended only temporarily in the liquid. You can separate the liquid from the large solid particles in a suspension by letting the particles settle and then by pouring off the liquid as shown in the illustration. This method of separation is called *decanting*. If a suspension contains very small particles, it may take days or weeks to settle. Decanting either isn't practical or won't work with these mixtures. Instead, you can separate the particles by pouring the mixture through a strainer or filter. Filtration can also be used to determine the size of the suspended particles.

Do the next experiment to discover more about suspensions and the way they are handled by scientists.

BORSCHT COCKTAIL: SEPARATING SUSPENDED PARTICLES

A *puree* is a suspension of food particles in a liquid. Purees are made with food processors or blenders or by pushing soft food through a strainer. Usually the pureed food particles are so small that they take a long time to settle. Pea soup, tomato sauce, and applesauce are examples of purees. Jarred beet soup, or borscht, is good for beginning a study of suspensions involving a beet puree.

Materials & Equipment

- ✦ a jar of borscht
- ✦ I tablespoon sour cream
- ✦ a watch with a second hand
- ✦ a strainer

- ✦ 2 glass jars
- ✦ some coffee filters
- ✦ a large spoon
- ✦ a wire whisk or an eggbeater

Procedure

1 Shake the jar of borscht. Use the watch to time how long it takes for the beet particles to settle on the bottom. Do some beet particles stay suspended longer than others? Which ones stay suspended longer?

2 Pour about a cup of the settled liquid through a strainer into a glass jar.

Observations

Are any beet particles caught by the strainer? What is the size of particles that pass through the

strainer? Are they smaller or larger than the holes in the strainer?

Procedure

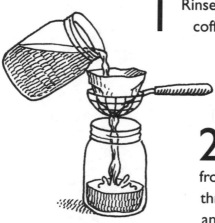

1 Rinse out the strainer. Put a coffee filter in the bottom of the strainer and place it over the second glass jar.

2 Pour the liquid you have just strained from the first glass jar through the filter paper and let the mixture drip through.

Observations

What evidence do you have that the filter paper has holes even though you can't see them? Are there any beet particles on the filter paper? Are these particles smaller or larger than the holes in the filter paper?

Taste the liquid that you have just filtered. Is there sugar in borscht? How can you tell? (Confirm your observations by reading the list of ingredients on the label.) What can you say about the size of

sugar particles compared to the size of the (too small to see) holes in the filter paper?

Procedure

1 Remove the filter paper from the strainer. Take 2 large spoonfuls of beets from the bottom of the jar of borscht. Push them through the strainer with a spoon into the liquid in the glass jar. Be sure to scrape the beets off the outside of the strainer. You can use some of the liquid from the jar you are straining into to wash the pureed beets through the strainer.

2 Stir or shake the pureed beets into the liquid.

Observations

How long does it take these particles to settle? Do they all settle eventually? How does the settling time compare with the time for the pieces of beet

before they were pureed? (If you find it difficult to see the beets, work in front of a strong light.)

From the results of your experiment, can you explain how settling rates and filtering can be used to find the size of particles? Can you think of how these procedures can be used to identify different substances as well as to separate them? Can you design an experiment to test the speeds on a blender or the blades on a food processor by creating purees with coarser and finer particles?

You can make a delicious cold soup with your experiment. Chill the pureed mixture. Beat in about a tablespoon of sour cream with a whisk or an eggbeater.

LIQUID FOOD AND THE TYNDALL EFFECT

Solutions and suspensions are both mixtures with two phases. One phase, the solvent, can be thought of as *continuous*. That is, all the particles are in contact with each other. The second phase, the solute, can be thought of as *discontinuous*. The solute particles are separated from each other by the solvent. The main difference between true solutions and suspensions is the size of the particles of the solute phase. In a solution, solute particles are approximately the size of single molecules. In a suspension, the particles are made up of countless numbers of molecules and are large enough to be filterable.

SOLUTION

A colloid is a third kind of mixture with two phases. The suspended particles in a colloid are larger than single molecules but small enough to remain in suspension permanently and be homogeneous. It is hard to tell the difference between a colloid and a solution just by looking at them. There is, however, a

SUSPENSION

COLLOID

simple test that does tell the difference. All you need is a clear glass and a flashlight.

If you pass a beam of light through a colloid, and you look at the beam from the side, you can see the beam. This is because the particles in a colloid are large enough to act as tiny mirrors and reflect light. This light-scattering ability is called the *Tyndall effect*. You can see the Tyndall effect in a beam of sunlight in a dusty room or from car headlights on a foggy night. Fog and dust particles are large enough to reflect light while air molecules are too small.

You can see the Tyndall effect in liquids we drink. Pour a small sample of a liquid into a clear glass. Hold the glass against a dark background and shine a flashlight beam through it. (A pen flashlight works especially well.) Look at the beam from the side. If you can see the beam as it passes through, the liquid is a colloid. If you can't see the beam from the side, the liquid is a solution.

Which of the following liquids are colloids and which are solutions? Tea, cranberry juice, syrup (colorless), orange drink (not juice), coffee, salt water, Jell-O, Kool-Aid, consommé, vinegar (distilled), egg white, cider.

Protoplasm, the living material of all cells, is a complicated colloid. What would you expect if you shone a beam of light through a cell?

SALAD DRESSING:
A LIQUID SUSPENDED IN A LIQUID

If you shake oil and water together and then let them stand, they will separate into two layers. Liquids that do not form solutions are said to be *immiscible*.

Classic French salad dressing (or vinaigrette) is a mixture of oil and vinegar and seasoning. Vinegar is a water-based substance (an acid) and is immiscible with oil. In order for all the flavors of the dressing to be evenly spread through a salad, it must be thoroughly mixed. A vinaigrette is usually given a number of hard shakes and immediately poured on a salad before the two liquids have a chance to separate.

This experiment is designed to answer the question: Does the size of the droplets of two immiscible liquids affect the rate of separation into layers?

Materials & Equipment

+ ⅓ cup vinegar
+ ½ teaspoon salt
+ ¼ teaspoon pepper
+ ¼ teaspoon garlic powder
+ ¼ teaspoon paprika
+ 1 cup salad oil
+ measuring cups and spoons

- ✦ a jar with a tight cover
- ✦ watch or clock with a second hand
- ✦ a small bowl
- ✦ an eggbeater or electric mixer
- ✦ a magnifying glass

Procedure

1 Put the vinegar in the jar and add the salt, pepper, garlic powder, and paprika. Screw the lid on tight and shake.

2 Pour in the salad oil and let the mixture stand for a few minutes.

Observations

Where does the oil go? Which do you think would be heavier, a cup of water or a cup of oil? Can you think of a way to check your guess?

Procedure

1 Cover the jar and shake about 10 times. Use the watch to see how long it takes for the mixture to separate. Can you see which is the continuous phase and which is the discontinuous?

2 Shake the jar hard about 20 times. Does the dressing take more or less time to separate? Look for droplets of vinegar suspended in the oil.

3 Shake the jar different numbers of times and examine the size of the droplets immediately

after shaking. When does the dressing have the smallest droplets?

4 Put the mixture in a small bowl and beat hard for about 4 minutes with an eggbeater or an electric mixer. Quickly pour the dressing back into the jar. Examine the droplets with a magnifying glass. How long does the dressing take to separate into two layers? What did shaking and beating do to the size of the droplets?

You can use the French dressing over a tossed green salad. Mix well and use just enough to coat the leaves lightly.

EMULSIONS

If milk, fresh from a cow, is allowed to stand, the fat rises to the top as cream. When milk is homogenized, it is forced through tiny holes in a screen.

This breaks up the butterfat into very tiny droplets. Why doesn't the butterfat separate from milk when it is homogenized?

A suspension of two immiscible liquids that doesn't separate on standing is called an *emulsion*. The word *emulsion* comes from a Latin word that means "to milk out." Emulsions have a milky or cloudy appearance. Cream is an emulsion in which droplets of butterfat are suspended in a water-based continuous phase. The watery part of milk or cream contains some milk proteins and sugar. If you put heavy cream into a jar with a tight cover and shake hard for a few minutes, you will produce the opposite result from the French dressing. When you make French dressing, shaking causes the discontinuous phase (the vinegar) to break up into tiny droplets and disperse throughout the continuous phase (the oil). If you shake heavy cream, you cause the tiny droplets of butterfat (the discontinuous phase) to come in contact with each other. This will be explored in the next chapter when you make butter.

MAYONNAISE: A STABILIZED EMULSION

When oil and vinegar in French dressing separate,

the vinegar droplets grow larger and larger, and the oil droplets grow larger and larger. The large oil droplets float to the surface of the vinegar. If, however, you add a certain third substance to a mixture of oil and vinegar, you can stabilize the mixture and prevent the separation. The result is a stable emulsion of two immiscible liquids and the substance that keeps the two liquids from separating is called an *emulsifying agent*.

One example of an emulsifying agent is soap. When you wash greasy dishes, hot water turns the grease into an oil. One end of a soap molecule attaches to the grease and the other end is soluble in water. Each grease droplet is held in suspension in the water by countless soap molecules. The emulsified grease is easily washed down the drain. Try washing greasy dishes in cold water and in hot water without soap to see how emulsifying by soap works. Can you get the dishes clean?

Mayonnaise is an emulsion of oil in vinegar. Vinegar is an acid in water. In the process of making mayonnaise, you disperse five parts oil into only one part water. The vinegar forms a thin coating around the oil droplets. The emulsifying agent is egg yolks. Making mayonnaise is a real challenge to many who pride themselves on being good cooks, but it is not difficult to make if you understand what is happening as the emulsion forms.

Materials & Equipment

- ✦ 2 egg yolks (see pages 197–98 for how to separate eggs)
- ✦ ½ teaspoon prepared mustard
- ✦ ½ teaspoon salt
- ✦ 3 tablespoons vinegar
- ✦ 1 cup salad oil
- ✦ measuring cups and spoons
- ✦ a small bowl
- ✦ an electric mixer or a friend and an eggbeater

Procedure

Have all the ingredients at room temperature. Cold oil does not flow as quickly as warmer oil, and cold egg yolks will not emulsify as much oil as warmer egg yolks. (Can you think of experiments to check these ideas out?)

I Put the egg yolks, mustard, salt, and 1 teaspoon of the vinegar in the bowl and beat at a medium speed until the egg yolks are lemon-colored. The egg yolks are now thoroughly mixed with the water in the vinegar and are ready to receive the oil.

2 Add the oil drop by drop while beating constantly. If you do not have an electric mixer, you can make the emulsion by hand with a friend. One of you does the beating with an eggbeater while the other adds oil.

The idea in making mayonnaise is to spread tiny droplets of oil evenly through the egg yolks. Egg yolk coats these droplets as they form and prevents them from coming together and forming a separate layer. If you add the oil too fast, or too much oil at one time, the droplets will come together before they can be forced into the egg yolks and the mayonnaise will "curdle" or separate. If this happens, you can correct the situation with a fresh egg yolk, but add the curdled mayonnaise to the yolk rather than the other way around.

You can tell when the emulsion has formed because the mixture gets thick. This usually happens after about one third of a cup of oil has been added.

3 Once the emulsion has formed, you can add the oil slightly faster until the full cup has been beaten into the yolks. If the mixture gets too thick, add a teaspoon of vinegar. Beat in the remaining vinegar at the end.

Homemade mayonnaise is thick, yellow, and

glistening. It spoils easily and should be stored in the refrigerator. Cover it so a skin doesn't form on top.

Several cookbooks make the claim that mayonnaise is difficult to make on a rainy day or when a thunderstorm is threatening. But mayonnaise is made commercially on every working day regardless of the weather. You might want to do some experiments to check this out.

STRAWBERRY BOMBE: A FROZEN EMULSION

Ice cream, bombes, and other frozen desserts contain water and cream. Separation of the fat in cream is not a problem because the fat droplets are very small. In frozen desserts the problem is to keep the water droplets small. Large water droplets form large ice crystals and give the dessert a grainy texture. As long as the ice crystals are tiny, the dessert will be smooth.

Suppose an emulsifying agent that attracts water is an ingredient in a frozen dessert. Do you think it can keep large ice crystals from forming as egg yolks keep large oil droplets from forming in mayonnaise? Discover the answer by making the strawberry bombe in the next experiment.

Materials & Equipment

- 1 teaspoon unflavored gelatin
- 4½ tablespoons cold water
- 1 9- or 10-ounce package frozen strawberries, defrosted
- 1 cup sugar
- 2 teaspoons lemon juice
- 1½ tablespoons boiling water
- 2 cups heavy or whipping cream
- measuring cups and spoons
- a small dish or cup
- 3 small bowls
- a spoon
- pen and labels
- an electric mixer or eggbeater
- a rubber spatula
- 2 1-pint containers (plastic ice-cream containers are good)

Procedure

1 Put the gelatin in the small dish or cup and add 1½ tablespoons cold water.

Does the gelatin attract water? How can you tell? You may have to wait a few minutes before you can answer these questions.

2 Put the strawberries in one of the bowls and add the sugar and lemon juice. Mix well and then pour half of the strawberry mixture into a second bowl.

3 When the gelatin has softened and absorbed all the cold water, add 1½ tablespoons of boiling water and stir until all the gelatin dissolves. Add the gelatin mixture to one of the strawberry mixtures and stir well. Stir 3 tablespoons of cold water into the other strawberry mixture as a control. Label the bowls so you know which one contains the gelatin.

4 Refrigerate the strawberry mixtures until the gelatin starts to thicken. It should not be firm but only slightly gelled. Start checking after 15 minutes. When the gelatin mixture is ready, remove it from the refrigerator.

5 In the third bowl whip the cream until it stands in soft peaks when you raise the beaters. Put half the whipped cream into each strawberry mixture.

6 Gently combine the strawberries and cream by using a rubber spatula to bring the mixture from the bottom of the bowl to the top. Repeat this motion again and again, until the whipped cream and strawberries are well mixed. (This is what is known as folding two ingredients together.)

7 Pour one strawberry-and-cream mixture into each pint container. Be sure to label the one containing the gelatin. Put the containers into the freezer for about 12 hours. When the desserts are frozen, taste them.

Observations

Is there a difference in texture between the dessert containing gelatin and the one without?

Let a few tablespoons of each dessert thaw and then refreeze them. Which dessert has a grainier texture? What do you think the gelatin does in a strawberry bombe?

CONSOMMÉ:
CLARIFICATION BY FLOCCULATION

Canned broths and bouillon cubes are staple foods in almost every kitchen. But true chefs pride themselves on their "stock pots," the broths they create with leftovers from daily food preparation. It takes time to create a broth—hours of simmering on the

stove. Broths are cloudy with all kinds of suspended particles. They are complicated suspensions and colloids with many kinds of particles in the discontinuous phase. A true bouillon or consommé is clear and sparkling. The word *bouillon* comes from the French word for *boil*. The word *consommé* comes from a word that means the *highest*. In the next experiment, you create your own broth and clarify it—that is, remove the particles—to make consommé. The project takes two days to complete. It will give you a real appreciation for homemade stock, and also for inexpensive, easy-to-use canned consommés and bouillon cubes. It will also show you a method for removing particles that is often used in many chemical industries.

Materials & Equipment

To make the broth:

+ 1 pound of lean sliced beef
+ about a pound of beef bones
+ water
+ 2 peeled carrots
+ 2 peeled onions
+ 2 stalks celery with leaves
+ 2 teaspoons salt

+ 6 sprigs fresh parsley
+ ¼ teaspoon thyme
+ 2 washed leeks
+ a 4-quart soup pot
+ a slotted spoon
+ a 2-quart bowl or container
+ a knife

Procedure

1 Put the meat and bones in the soup pot and add enough cold water to fill the pot about $^3/_4$ full. Set the pot over low to medium heat. As the liquid starts to simmer, a scum will rise to the surface. Skim it off with a slotted spoon until it stops forming. This will take about 5 minutes. It is important not to let the soup boil violently, as the scum will be returned to the broth and make it even more cloudy.

2 Add the rest of the ingredients and let the mixture simmer uncovered for at least 4 hours. The liquid will be reduced by about half.

3 Remove all the solid ingredients from the broth. They are good to eat. Pour the broth into a bowl or container. Notice that the liquid fat rises to the surface. Refrigerate uncovered overnight.

4 The next day the fat will be a hard, whitish layer on top of the broth. Remove it by cutting around the edge with a knife to separate it from the wall of the container. The whole layer of fat can be lifted out in one piece. Fish out any remaining pieces of fat with a slotted spoon. Notice how cloudy the broth is. You're going to get rid of the cloudiness with a very amazing procedure using egg whites. This is the clarification procedure.

Materials & Equipment

- ✦ 2 egg whites
- ✦ ½ of the cold stock, about 1 quart
- ✦ 2 crushed eggshells
- ✦ a small bowl
- ✦ a wire whisk
- ✦ a 2-quart saucepan
- ✦ colander
- ✦ cheesecloth
- ✦ a large bowl
- ✦ a spoon
- ✦ a ladle

The large bowl must be one that the colander can rest in with its bottom well above the bottom of the bowl.

Procedure

I Beat the egg whites slightly with a wire whisk in a small bowl. Put 1 quart of your stock in a saucepan and beat in the egg whites with the whisk. Add the crushed eggshells. Place the saucepan over low heat, and slowly, without stirring, let the soup come to a simmer so that it is barely moving. **Do not let the soup boil, or the egg white will break up and fail to clarify the soup.** The egg white and shells float to the surface of the soup, forming a "raft" that is strengthened by the eggshell pieces. The egg white is *coagulating* (more on this in Chapter 5, "Proteins") and becoming firm due to the heat. Amazingly it acts like a magnet for some

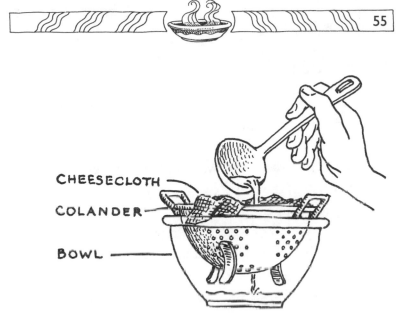

CHEESECLOTH

COLANDER

BOWL

of the larger particles floating in the broth. This process of drawing out impurities by collecting them in bunches is called *flocculation*. (Stump your folks at the dinner table with that word tonight.) Carefully simmer your broth for about 15 minutes. Remove from the heat and allow it to cool, undisturbed, for about an hour.

2 Line the colander with 8 layers of wet and wrung-out cheesecloth. Set it above the large bowl. Gently push the raft to one side with a spoon and carefully ladle the broth into the cheesecloth, which will filter out any egg white and eggshell particles.

Observations

Compare the clarified broth with the original broth. If you made a mistake and boiled the egg white mixture, you can chill it and try the process again with fresh egg whites. You can clarify the other half of the broth or not, as you wish. It is perfectly good to eat unclarified.

Taste your consommé. If it is not as strong as you might like, add a bouillon cube or two. You can add cooked noodles or vegetables or meat to create any number of soups from your consommé. Eat and enjoy.

Carbohdyrates and Fats

Solutions, suspensions, and emulsions are all mixtures that can be separated and purified into simpler substances. One question that challenged scientists was: What are the simplest substances of all? It turns out that there are only two kinds of pure substances on earth: *compounds* and *elements*.

Elements are the simplest kinds of pure matter. Ninety-two elements have been identified in the earth's crust and a number of others have been made in laboratories. The most common elements found in food (and that also make up your body) are carbon, hydrogen, oxygen, and nitrogen. Living

things also contain sulfur, phosphorus, iron, magnesium, sodium, potassium, and chlorine, to name a few.

It took a long time to discover all of the elements. This is because elements combine to form compounds, and it was hard to tell whether a pure substance was an element or if it was a compound. Water is a good example. Water is an extremely stable compound, and it takes enormous amounts of energy to break it up into its elements. So for hundreds of years, people thought that water was an element. It was a great scientific breakthrough when water was found to be a compound made of hydrogen and oxygen, two substances known to be elements.

Elements combine to form compounds very differently from the way substances combine to form mixtures. The properties of the components of mixtures don't change as a result of being part of a mixture. But most compounds have very different properties from the elements that are its components. (Think how water is different from oxygen and hydrogen. Hydrogen is an explosive gas. Oxygen is also a gas, and it supports burning and life. Water is a liquid at ordinary temperatures and neither burns nor supports burning.) Compounds are also made of fixed amounts of combined elements. Any amount of hydrogen and oxygen can be mixed together, but water forms from two parts of hydrogen and one part of oxygen. Any extra hydrogen or oxygen present from the original mixture will be left over after water has formed.

Sugars and *starches* are compounds that are important kinds of food. They are made of only three elements—carbon, hydrogen, and oxygen. When sugars and starches are broken down into these elements, there are two atoms of hydrogen and one of oxygen for every atom of carbon. Two atoms of hydrogen and one atom of oxygen are the same as a molecule of water. For this reason, sugars and starches were called *carbohydrates*, which means "watered carbon." This chapter investigates some of the properties of this interesting group of compounds.

SYRUPS:
SOLUTIONS THAT DON'T CRYSTALLIZE

One property of sugar is that it dissolves in water. If it didn't, you couldn't make rock candy. Actually, making rock candy involves recovering solute crystals from solution, not dissolving them. Corn syrup, molasses, maple syrup, and honey are all examples

of sugar solutions. Do the next experiment to see if you can recover sugar crystals from these solutions.

Pour a small amount of each syrup into small shallow dishes and let them stand for several days. In some cases no crystals will form and you will be left with a thick, sticky material in the bottom of the dish. Scientists are always looking for testable questions, ones that can be answered by experimenting. Answering the question "Why don't sugar crystals form from some syrups?" could lead to other testable questions.

Perhaps the syrups are not reaching the supersaturated condition necessary for crystallization to occur. Does syrup absorb water from the air even while water is evaporating from its surface so that most of the sugar remains in solution?

To test this idea make a supersaturated sugar solution as for rock candy (see Chapter 2, pages 13–14). Divide the solution into two dishes. Leave one dish exposed to the air and cover the other with a cake cover or large glass bowl. Before you cover the second dish, sprinkle some calcium chloride on the table around it. Calcium chloride absorbs moisture from the air and will keep the air above the dish dry. You can get calcium chloride in hobby shops.

Perhaps crystals form more slowly from solu-

tions containing several solutes than from a solution containing only one solute?

Materials & Equipment

- ◆ 1½ cups water
- ◆ 2 cups sugar
- ◆ 7½ tablespoons white corn syrup
- ◆ ½ teaspoon cream of tartar
- ◆ a saucepan with a cover
- ◆ a wooden spoon
- ◆ a candy thermometer
- ◆ 3 foil dishes

Procedure

1 Put ½ cup water, ⅔ cup sugar, 2½ table-spoons corn syrup, and ¼ teaspoon cream of tartar into the saucepan and stir over medium heat until dissolved. When the mixture starts to boil, cover it briefly so that the steam washes all the sugar crystallized on the side of the saucepan back into the solution.

2 Uncover and put in the candy thermometer.

Continue to boil without stirring until the temperature reaches 290°F (143°C). Carefully pour the syrup into a foil dish.

3 & 4 Make two more batches of syrup with new ingredients and these small variations: In the second batch, leave out the cream of tartar. In the third batch, use the cream of tartar but heat the mixture only until all the sugar is dissolved. As the solutions cool, you can tell when crystals have formed because the solution becomes cloudy. Close examination with a magnifying glass will reveal thousands of tiny, needlelike crystals.

Observations

Where do crystals form? They should form in two of the syrup batches, while one should remain clear.

There are a number of different kinds of sugars. All are sweet and they all dissolve in water. Some sugars contain only five or six carbon atoms per molecule. These are called simple sugars, and they include *glucose* (sometimes called dextrose) from beets, *fructose* from fruit, and *lactose* from milk. Table sugar is called *sucrose*. It is not a simple sugar because each sucrose molecule is a two-molecule chain of one fructose molecule and one glucose molecule linked together.

When a sucrose solution is heated to a high temperature, it begins to break down into glucose and fructose. This breakdown is speeded up with the addition of an acid such as cream of tartar. The result is a syrup containing a mixture of three sugar solutes—glucose, fructose, and sucrose. Crystals will not form in such a mixture because a crystal is the result of a regular arrangement of identical molecules. When there are several different kinds of molecules in a solution, similar molecules have a harder time getting together.

The syrups you have made can be poured over ice cream or popcorn.

HYGROSCOPIC COOKIES

Ever notice how cookies lose their crispness when they've been exposed to air for a while? Cookie manufacturers have. That's why they seal their products in packages that keep them from being exposed to water vapor in the air. The ingredient in cookies that is chiefly responsible for absorbing moisture is sugar. Such a substance is described as *hygroscopic*, which means "wet looking."

Is one kind of sugar more hygroscopic than another? The next experiment compares cookies made with granulated sucrose and those made with honey. Taste honey and sugar. Which is sweeter?

Materials & Equipment

- ✦ 2 cups flour
- ✦ 1 teaspoon baking powder
- ✦ ½ teaspoon salt
- ✦ 1 stick (½ cup) unsalted butter
- ✦ ½ cup sugar
- ✦ 1 egg
- ✦ 2 tablespoons water
- ✦ ½ teaspoon lemon juice
- ✦ ¼ cup honey

- ✦ measuring cups and spoons
- ✦ a flour sifter
- ✦ a fork
- ✦ 4 bowls
- ✦ electric mixer or eggbeater
- ✦ waxed paper
- ✦ greased cookie sheets
- ✦ a metal spatula
- ✦ wire cooling racks

Procedure

1 Preheat the oven to 400°F. Sift 2 cups of flour onto waxed paper. Measure out 1 cup of this sifted flour and resift it together with ½ teaspoon baking powder and ¼ teaspoon salt into a bowl.

Resift a second cup of flour with ½ teaspoon baking powder and ¼ teaspoon salt into a second bowl. Set dry ingredients aside.

2 Put ½ stick of softened butter into a third bowl. Beat until creamy with an electric mixer or eggbeater. Add ½ cup of sugar to the butter and continue beating until thoroughly mixed.

3 Beat the egg with a fork in a measuring cup. Put half the egg into the butter-sugar mixture. Also add 1 of the bowls of dry ingredients, water, and lemon juice. Blend until smooth.

4 Now prepare the batter with honey. Put the remaining ½ stick of softened butter in a fourth bowl and beat until creamy. Beat in the honey. Add the other half of the egg and the second bowl of dry ingredients to the butter-honey mixture. You do not need to put in lemon juice, as honey already contains an acid. Mix until well blended.

5 Drop small spoonfuls of the batter onto greased cookie sheets, leaving about 2 inches between cookies. Bake until brown around the edges, about 7 minutes. Be sure to keep track of which cookies contain sugar and which contain honey.

Let the cookies cool for a few minutes on the sheets before moving them to a wire rack with a metal spatula. When they are completely cool, store the cookies in airtight containers.

Observations

When they are cool, eat a sugar cookie and a honey cookie. Are they about the same crispness? Are they the same color? Which is browner? Leave one of each kind of cookie exposed to the air. Take a bite of each every few hours. Which cookie loses its crispness more quickly? If you wanted to make a cake that would stay moist for a long time, what might you use to keep it moist?

STARCHES

Sucrose is a two-molecule chain of simple sugars. A starch molecule is made of long chains of simple sugar molecules. Plants make starch molecules as a way of storing sugar because it can be easily converted back to sugar when needed. If you have any doubt that starch is made of sugar, an experiment using a chemical made by your own body can give you the answer. Do the following experiment and see for yourself.

Materials & Equipment

+ a soda cracker, saltine, or other plain flour cracker

+ your tastebuds

Procedure

A soda cracker is made of flour (a starch), water, and baking powder. It contains no sugar. Check the ingredients listed on the box to make sure. Chew a soda cracker well and hold it in your mouth, without swallowing, for 5 minutes.

Observations

Does the taste of the soda cracker change? There is a special chemical in your saliva that breaks the links in the starch chains so that sugar molecules are released. You should be able to taste this change.

Compare some of the properties of starches and sugars. How is the taste different? Try putting different starches in water. In addition to flour, common starches include arrowroot starch, cornstarch, and potato starch. Which dissolves most easily? In general, smaller molecules dissolve more easily than larger molecules. Sugar dissolves more easily than starch.

Like sugar, starches also absorb water. When starches are heated with water, they swell. This property, called *gelatinization*, makes them very useful as thickeners for sauces and gravies.

Many different foods contain starch. There is a

simple chemical test for starch. Put a few drops of iodine solution (called tincture of iodine, available in most drugstores) on the food. If starch is present, the iodine changes from reddish-brown to a blue-black. **Don't eat any food on which you put iodine! Iodine is poisonous.**

TAPIOCA

Tapioca is a starch that comes from the root of a Brazilian cassava plant. Cassava flour is rolled into little balls, which are sold as dried "pearls." Tapioca pearls are used to make thick puddings.

Put a drop of iodine on a tapioca pearl. Does it give a positive starch test? Discard the pearl you tested. Take $\frac{1}{4}$ cup of tapioca pearls and put them in $\frac{3}{4}$ cup of water. Let them soak for 12 hours. How does the size of the soaked tapioca compare with dried pearls? How is this evidence that starches swell with water?

Make tapioca pudding with the soaked pearls.

Materials & Equipment

+ $\frac{1}{4}$ cup tapioca pearls soaked in $\frac{3}{4}$ cup water
+ $2\frac{1}{4}$ cups milk
+ $\frac{1}{4}$ teaspoon salt
+ water
+ 2 eggs
+ $\frac{1}{2}$ cup sugar

- ✦ I teaspoon vanilla
- ✦ a double boiler
- ✦ a wooden spoon
- ✦ 4 dessert cups
- ✦ measuring cups and spoons
- ✦ a small bowl
- ✦ an eggbeater
- ✦ plastic wrap

Procedure

I Test a small sample of milk, salt, eggs, sugar, and vanilla for starch. **Don't use any of the ingredients you have tested when you are preparing the pudding.** Is starch present in any of these ingredients?

2 Put the soaked pearls in the top of a double boiler with the milk and the salt. Fill the bottom of the double boiler about three quarters full with water and set over medium heat. Cook the tapioca mixture, uncovered, over boiling water for about an hour, stirring occasionally with a wooden spoon.

3 In a small bowl, beat the eggs with the sugar. Mix a few spoonfuls of the hot tapioca mixture into the egg-sugar mixture. This will warm up the eggs slowly. If you were

to put the eggs directly into the hot tapioca mixture, they would cook and you'd have scrambled eggs in your tapioca.

Add the warmed egg-sugar mixture to the tapioca in the pot. Cook about 3 minutes more.

4 Remove the double boiler from the stove, and set the top aside to cool for 15 minutes. Then mix in the vanilla. Divide the pudding into four dessert dishes, cover with plastic wrap, and chill.

5 Test part of the pudding (not a pearl) for starch. Then pick out a pearl from the pudding, wash it off and test it for starch. What has happened to some of the starch that was in the tapioca pearls? What has this starch done to the liquid milk? Again, **don't eat** anything that has iodine on it.

GRAPE JELLY: HOW PECTIN ACTS

Pectin is a starch found in especially high amounts in green apples and the white underskin of citrus fruits. When pectin is cooked with sugar and acid, it swells to form a clear, thick jelly.

Pectin is prepared commercially and is sold in a package with an acid. Is the added sugar necessary for the formation of a firm jelly? Or can a pectin-acid combo do it alone? That's what the next experiment is designed to find out.

Materials & Equipment

+ 3 cups sugar
+ 1 6-ounce can of grape juice concentrate (thawed)
+ 2 cups water
+ 1 package of Sure-Jell (commercially prepared pectin and acid)
+ measuring cups and spoons

+ a large saucepan
+ a wooden spoon
+ 4 6-ounce glasses or jelly jars
+ a metal spoon
+ melted paraffin for sealing off the jelly jars (not necessary if you will eat all the jelly within two weeks)

Procedure

1 Put 3 ounces of juice concentrate, 1 cup of water, and ½ package of Sure-Jell (2½ tablespoons) in a saucepan. Cook over high heat, stirring constantly, until bubbles form all around the edge.

2 Add 1 cup sugar all at once and stir. Bring the mixture to a rolling boil and allow it to boil without stirring for 1 minute.

3 Remove from the heat. Use a metal spoon to skim the scum that rises off the surface. Pour into two glasses. If you plan to store the jelly, pour melted paraffin on top to seal it closed. Sealed jelly doesn't need to be refrigerated. Unsealed does.

4 Make a second batch of jelly with the remaining Sure-Jell, juice concentrate, and water, and this time use 2 cups of sugar.

Observations

Which jelly is firmer? The softer jelly makes a good sauce for vanilla ice cream.

FATS AND OILS

Most of the compounds found in living organisms are made up of only a few of the 92 naturally occurring elements. Carbon, hydrogen, and oxygen are found in a countless number of compounds. The differences in these compounds are due to the amounts of each element that are present and the way the atoms are arranged in the molecules.

Fats and oils, like carbohydrates, are a group of compounds made of only carbon, hydrogen, and oxygen. Fats and oils are produced by animals and plants as a method of storing food. Molecules of sugars and starches become fat or oil molecules as the atoms are rearranged. Stored fats and oils protect an organism against a time when food is scarce.

You can find out if a food contains fat or oil by rubbing it on a piece of brown paper bag. If the food contains a greasy substance, a translucent spot (an area that lets light through) will appear where you have rubbed. Water in food will also produce a translucent spot, but a water spot disappears when the water dries. A fat or oil spot will not disappear.

Animal fats, such as butter or lard, are usually solids at room temperature, while vegetable fats are liquids. Vegetable oils can be made into solid fats in a laboratory by adding hydrogen gas under pressure. The terms *saturated* and *unsaturated* fats refer to the amount of hydrogen in a fat. Saturated fats contain more hydrogen than unsaturated or polyunsaturated fats. Saturated fats are usually solid, while unsaturated fats are oils. Margarine, which is advertised as being made from oil, contains some saturated fat. Hydrogen was added to make the fat solid.

There is a discussion among scientists about whether eating certain kinds of fat may affect your health. When some people age, yellowish, fatty deposits of a substance called *cholesterol* form inside the arteries, leaving a narrower passage for blood to get through. This condition, called arteriosclerosis,

can cause blood clots, which may block an artery and cause it to burst. It may also completely close an artery, cutting off the blood supply to a part of the body. If this happens in one of the arteries that nourishes the heart or brain, death can result. Some scientists claim that saturated fats in the diet may increase the amount of cholesterol in the body, and unsaturated fats may lower blood-cholesterol levels. For this reason, doctors suggest that older people cut down on the amounts of butter, cheese, and fatty meats in their diets.

NUT BUTTER:
PRESSING OUT OILS

Nuts contain oil, and oil burns easily with a steady flame. See for yourself by setting a Brazil nut or an almond on fire. Set the nut in the center of a pan. Hold a wooden match to the end of the nut until it burns steadily. You can toast a marshmallow in the nut's flame.

Many vegetable oils are prepared by crushing olives, seeds, or nuts in presses. The oil is then separated from the nuts or seeds. In the next experiment, you will release the oil in nuts. Since it is difficult to separate the oil without the proper

equipment, you will create a mixture of oil and nuts—a nut butter—that is good to eat.

Materials & Equipment

- ✦ ½ to 1 cup shelled almonds, pecans, or walnuts
- ✦ a nut grinder or food processor
- ✦ 2 plastic bags
- ✦ a rolling pin
- ✦ a spatula
- ✦ a jar with a lid

Procedure

You can use pecans or walnuts as they come out of the shell, but almonds should be white with their outer skins removed. This is done by putting shelled almonds into boiling water for a few minutes. Drain them and let them cool. They almost pop out of their skins if your hold them at the broad end and squeeze gently.

1 Put the nuts through a nut grinder or grind in a food processor. If you haven't got either of these tools, put the nuts in a double plastic bag and pound them with a rolling pin. You are trying to break up the nuts into the smallest possible pieces.

2 After the nuts are ground, put them into a plastic bag and roll the rolling pin on them with as much pressure as possible. (Hydraulic presses are used commercially to extract oil from

olives and peanuts.) The nut particles will begin to cling together as the oil is pressed from the nut meat. The finer the nut meat, the better the butter will be.

3 When the butter is as finely pressed as you can get it, scrape it into a jar. Store the nut butter, covered, in the refrigerator, as it spoils easily.

Nut butters can be used as spreads on bread and crackers. Try a nut butter and jelly sandwich for a variation on an old favorite.

BUTTER: COALESCING FAT DROPLETS FROM A SUSPENSION

Milk has often been called the most complete food. It contains water, carbohydrates, vitamins, minerals,

proteins, and fat. Butter is made by extracting the fat from the other parts of milk. Cream contains more butterfat than whole milk. Use it to make butter in the next experiment.

Materials & Equipment

+ ½ pint heavy cream
+ a pint jar with a tight cover
+ a marble

Procedure

1 Put the cream in the jar with the marble. Screw on the cover and make sure that there are no leaks.

2 Shake the jar in a figure-eight motion. At first you will hear the marble moving. Then there will be a time when the cream will be so thick that you won't be able to feel the marble

moving. Then, suddenly, the butter will form.

3 Drain the buttermilk—which is also good to drink—from the butter. Wash the butter by running cold tap water into the jar to remove any trapped buttermilk. Fish out the marble and pack the butter down. Store in the refrigerator.

Observations

The process of making butter takes advantage of certain properties of fat. When milk first comes from a cow, the butterfat is in the form of droplets that are suspended in the liquid. If fresh, whole milk is allowed to stand, fat droplets rise to the top, carrying along some liquid. This is cream, and it is less dense than the more watery part of the milk.

Cream is a fat-in-water emulsion. The fat droplets are held in suspension by milk proteins. The butter-making process is the formation of a water-in-fat emulsion where water droplets are suspended in the fat.

When you make butter from cream, you force the fat droplets to come together. They form larger and larger globules until they separate from the water part of the mixture. This process is called *coalescing*. Butterfat coalesces because the fat globules are more attracted to each other than they are to the water in which they are suspended. When you

shake the cream, you force the fat droplets to come into contact with each other. The marble stirs up the mixture as you shake it, increasing the opportunity of fat droplets from different parts of the mixture to come in contact with each other.

The amount of butterfat varies in cream. Light cream has much less butterfat than heavy cream. The amount of fat in cream is the most important factor in making good whipped cream. Try making whipped cream from heavy cream and light cream. Which whips more easily? Which keeps its stiffness longer?

AN ICE CREAM TASTE TEST

You may consider yourself an expert on ice cream, but do you really know a good ice cream when you taste it? Is there a real measurable difference between expensive premium brands and less expensive ice creams? How can you measure something that depends on personal opinion? The next experiment is designed to eliminate the variables that shape opinions. You will need a group of people to sample different ice creams and evaluate them. The larger the group the better, but even a group of five or six friends can give you some idea of which ice cream is the favorite.

Materials & Equipment

- 4 different kinds of vanilla ice cream:
  1 premium brand (The word "premium" must appear on the package. Usually it is expensive and sold in pint containers.)
  1 moderately priced brand that is also labeled "premium"
  1 very inexpensive brand
  1 ice milk or vanilla frozen yogurt
- 4 bowls
- labels and a pen

For each person taking the test:

- a spoon
- a glass of water
- a napkin
- a pencil or pen
- an Ice Cream Taste Test Data Sheet copied from this book

Procedure

If you are conducting this experiment, you cannot participate in the test. Here's the setup.

1 Put a different ice cream in each bowl and label the bowl with a number so only you can identify which ice cream it holds. Don't throw out the containers the ice cream came in, and also make a note of the prices paid for each brand.

2 Don't let the participants see the original containers. They should see only the ice cream in

the bowls at the time of the experiment. Packaging and brand names can have a large effect on how people "taste" ice creams.

Some of the other things that could influence how people perceive the different ice cream tastes are: conversation between participants, the order in which they taste the ice cream, and leftover flavor from the last ice cream tasted. So you must instruct your participants not to speak to or look at each other. They should take a sip of water between tastes, and sample each ice cream at least three or four times, in different orders, before drawing any conclusions.

Here are some of the things professional ice cream taste testers look for:

Color—The color should be what you expect for the flavor. Vanilla is not too yellow or too white.

Melting—The best ice cream melts quickly at room temperature, and the melted ice cream is a smooth liquid without foamy bubbles.

Body and texture—The best ice cream is firm but drips easily. The "mouth-feel" is creamy smooth and chewy. Better ice creams have more butterfat and stay firm at lower temperatures. They don't feel as cold as less expensive ice creams that have such a cold feel they can give you a headache.

Flavor—Vanilla ice cream should be pleasantly sweet and you should be able to taste the vanilla.

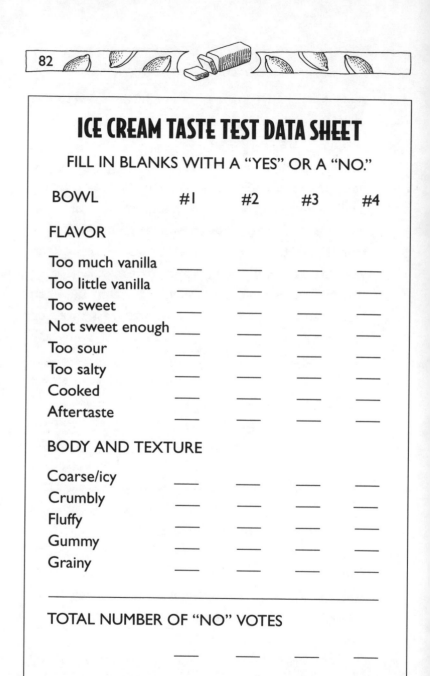

ICE CREAM TASTE TEST DATA SHEET

FILL IN BLANKS WITH A "YES" OR A "NO."

BOWL	#1	#2	#3	#4
FLAVOR				
Too much vanilla	___	___	___	___
Too little vanilla	___	___	___	___
Too sweet	___	___	___	___
Not sweet enough	___	___	___	___
Too sour	___	___	___	___
Too salty	___	___	___	___
Cooked	___	___	___	___
Aftertaste	___	___	___	___
BODY AND TEXTURE				
Coarse/icy	___	___	___	___
Crumbly	___	___	___	___
Fluffy	___	___	___	___
Gummy	___	___	___	___
Grainy	___	___	___	___

TOTAL NUMBER OF "NO" VOTES

___	___	___	___

The ice cream should not taste "cooked" like milk that has been boiled.

3 After all the tasters have finished collecting their own data, add up the total number of "no" votes for each ice cream for the group. The ice cream with the most no votes wins.

Observations

Which ice cream wins? Do people generally prefer the most expensive ice cream?

Look at the list of ingredients on the cartons. All ice cream contains butterfat (in cream), milk, sugar, flavoring, and air that has been beaten in. Premium ice creams have more fat and less air than cheaper ice creams. High fat content lets the ice cream remain firm at warmer temperatures. Premium ice creams melt without leaving behind a foam. Cheap ice creams have less fat and more air. Ice crystals tend to be larger, and the ice cream feels colder. Emulsifiers and stabilizers are added to keep the size of the ice crystals small, but they can give the product a sticky, gummy texture and a strange aftertaste. The temperature, texture, and mouth feel can tell you a lot about the ingredients. In general, premium ice creams have fewer ingredients than cheaper ice creams.

With practice, you can become a champion ice cream taster.

Proteins

In the eighteenth century scientists became interested in a substance, found in all living things, that acted differently from all other substances. When a fluid like blood or egg white was heated, it did not become a boiling liquid like water or oil. Instead, it became a solid. And, if this was not strange enough, once changed to a solid, it could never again be a liquid. Nothing could be done to return blood or egg white to its original liquid state. It did not take scientists long to realize that this strange material that changed permanently when heated was the very basis of all life. For this reason, they named it *protein* meaning "of first importance."

Proteins have turned out to be the most complicated and numerous of all the compounds found in living things. Some proteins, like egg white, dissolve in water; some, like hair, are fibers. Some, like muscle protein, are responsible for movement in animals. But all proteins have certain things in common. In addition to the elements carbon, hydrogen, and oxygen, all proteins contain nitrogen. The atoms of these elements, along with an occasional atom of sulfur, form small molecules called *amino acids*. Proteins are chains of amino acids.

Only 20 different amino acids make up most proteins. The different amino acids are like an alphabet for proteins. When you think of all you can say with 26 letters, you can see how 20 amino acids can be used to form so many different kinds of proteins. A protein molecule can be thought of as a chemical sentence or even a paragraph. And the proteins of each kind of organism can be thought of as being its own unique language.

When human beings and other animals digest food, what they are doing is breaking down the protein they have eaten into amino acids. The amino acids from food are reassembled to build new proteins that are the particular type for that organism.

Scientists have found protein to be one of the most challenging kinds of material to study. You can use some of their methods of investigation to learn how different kinds of protein behave and how

some of the properties of certain proteins are important in food preparation.

MERINGUES:
THE PROPERTIES OF EGG WHITE

An egg white is a good place to start learning about proteins. It is made up of about 87 percent water, a trace of minerals, and about 9 percent protein. The protein in an egg white makes it very useful for preparing food with different textures and consistencies.

Materials & Equipment

- ✦ 3 eggs
- ✦ water
- ✦ a knife
- ✦ a deep bowl
- ✦ a plastic ice cube tray
- ✦ plastic wrap
- ✦ 2 small transparent glasses
- ✦ a flashlight
- ✦ a spoon
- ✦ an electric mixer or eggbeater
- ✦ a magnifying glass

Procedure

Let the eggs come to room temperature. Protein in egg white is most useful to cooks at about 79°F (26°C). (You can check this out by try-

ing to make meringues from egg whites at different temperatures.)

Separate the whites from the yolks using the instructions on pages 197–98, putting the whites into a deep bowl. Save the yolks; you'll need them for the next experiment. Put each egg yolk in its own compartment of a plastic ice cube tray, leaving empty compartments between the yolks. Cover the tray with plastic wrap and refrigerate.

2 Pour enough egg white into a glass to make a depth of two inches. Shine a beam of light through the egg white. Can you see the beam as it passes through? The beam is an example of the Tyndall effect. What does it tell you about the size of the particles in egg white? (See Chapter 3, page 40 if you don't remember the Tyndall effect.) It has been proven that protein particles are single molecules. They are among the largest molecules in existence.

3 Pour the egg white back into the bowl. Put some water in the glass. Take about a teaspoon of egg white and stir it into the water. Does the egg white dissolve?

4 Beat the egg whites in the bowl with an electric mixer or eggbeater until they are foamy but will still flow if poured. Take about ½ teaspoon of foam and put it in a fresh glass of water. Does it

dissolve? What shape are the tiny particles that are suspended in the water? Use a magnifying glass.

Observations

You have just demonstrated a very important property of proteins. That is, that the shape of a protein molecule plays an important part in determining how it behaves. Protein molecules in egg whites are like tiny balls of yarn. Their round, compact shape enables them to dissolve in water. When you beat egg whites, you are, in effect, unraveling these balls of yarn. The long chains that form are too large to dissolve. The process of changing protein from its natural form is called *denaturing*. It is impossible to restore denatured egg white to its original form.

The egg whites can be used to make meringues, which show some other properties of proteins.

Materials & Equipment

+ oil
+ 3 egg whites, beaten foamy in previous experiment
+ ½ teaspoon cream of tartar
+ ½ teaspoon salt

+ ½ teaspoon vanilla extract
+ 1 cup superfine sugar
+ a cookie sheet
+ brown paper
+ a rubber spatula

+ measuring cups and spoons
+ an electric mixer or eggbeater
+ airtight container

Procedure

1 Preheat the oven to 175°F. Prepare a cookie sheet by covering it with brown paper rubbed with a little oil to coat.

2 Add the cream of tartar, salt, and vanilla extract to your foamy egg whites. Cream of tartar is an acid that makes the foam last longer. (You can test this idea with a simple side experiment. Beat two egg whites in separate bowls. Add ⅛ teaspoon cream of tartar to one egg white before you beat it. Find out which foam lasts longer.)

Beat the egg whites with an electric mixer or eggbeater until you can make peaks that stand upright. As the egg whites are beaten, the protein becomes more and more unraveled, and the foam becomes stiffer and stiffer.

3 Slowly add the sugar by sprinkling a tablespoon at a time over the egg whites. Continue beating while adding the sugar. Occasionally scrape down the sides of the bowl with a rubber spatula.

The water in the egg whites is carried along the

strands of protein. When sugar is beaten into stiff egg whites, it dissolves into this water. This is why you use superfine sugar (which dissolves more easily), and you add it very slowly to give it a chance to go into solution. If all the sugar doesn't dissolve, tiny droplets of sugar syrup will form on the surface of the finished product. Professional chefs consider such a "weeping" meringue a failure.

4 After you have added all the sugar, taste the meringue. It should not feel gritty, but if it does, beat in a tablespoon of water to dissolve all the sugar.

5 Make four separate piles of meringue on the oiled paper. Push down the middle of each pile to make a bowl shape.

6 The last step in making a meringue is to remove the water. This is accomplished by drying it in a warm oven for a long time.

Put the meringues in the oven for one hour at 175°F. At the end of that time, turn off the oven and

let the meringues stay in the oven overnight.

A successful meringue is a stiff, snow-white confection that will keep for weeks in an airtight container. (Since sugar absorbs moisture from the air, meringues must be stored away from the air. Otherwise, they become soft and fall apart.)

Fill the meringues with fruit or ice cream and top with whipped cream or chocolate sauce.

HOW TO SAVE EGG YOLKS

Egg yolks contain the nutrients needed to nourish a growing chick. Since they can also provide nourishment for countless bacteria, they are among the most perishable of leftovers. One way to preserve food is to freeze it. Water in frozen food is solid ice and is not available to microorganisms. But freezing can also make the yolk unusable unless you are an inventive chef. Do the next experiment to see if there is a way around this problem.

Materials & Equipment

- 3 egg yolks
- ⅛ teaspoon salt
- ⅛ teaspoon sugar
- a plastic ice cube tray
- measuring spoons
- a spoon
- paper
- a pencil
- plastic wrap
- a knife

Procedure

1 Take the egg yolks you saved from the last experiment out of the refrigerator. Put about ⅛ teaspoon salt in one egg yolk and stir it well with a spoon. Rinse off the spoon. Put about ⅛ teaspoon sugar in another egg yolk and stir. Rinse the spoon again and stir the third egg yolk, but don't put anything in it.

2 Draw a diagram of the ice cube tray showing where each egg yolk is located. Cover the tray with plastic wrap and put in the freezer overnight.

3 The next day, let the yolks defrost at room temperature. Stick a knife into each one (rinsing it off between dips). See whether the egg yolk is a firm semisolid or still runny. You can use the runny egg yolks to make cupcakes. The semisolid yolk is perfectly edible, but not too tasty.

Observations

The egg yolk is about half water. The solids are mostly fats and some proteins. Some proteins are dissolved in the watery phase of the egg yolk. But most of the yolk proteins and all of the fat are in tiny round particles that are suspended in the liquid creating a thick emulsion. When you hard-boil an egg, the soft, crumbly, grainy texture of the yolk is

due to the denaturing of the granular proteins.

When an egg yolk is frozen, the protein in the water solution is denatured, trapping the water and producing a solid mass when it is defrosted. If you add salt or sugar to an egg yolk, however, some of the water is removed from its close connection with protein. It is not trapped in the denatured protein after defrosting, so the eggs yolks remain runny.

A Quick Cupcake Recipe
Materials & Equipment

+ ½ stick butter, softened
+ ½ cup sugar
+ 2 egg yolks
+ 1 cup cake flour (not self-rising)
+ 1⅓ teaspoons baking powder
+ ¼ teaspoon salt
+ ⅓ cup milk
+ ¾ teaspoon vanilla
+ measuring cups and spoons
+ 2 medium bowls
+ a sifter
+ an electric mixer
+ a cupcake pan
+ cupcake liners

Procedure

Preheat the oven to 350°F. Beat the softened butter in a bowl with the sugar. Then beat in the egg yolks.

2 In another bowl sift together the cake flour, baking powder, and salt.

3 Pour the milk and the vanilla into a measuring cup. Add about one third of the dry ingredients to the butter-sugar mixture. Then beat in half of the milk mixture, then another third of the dry ingredients, then the rest of the milk, and then the rest of the dry ingredients. You should beat the batter well after each addition.

4 Line 4 baking cups with cupcake liners, pour the batter into them, and bake for 25–30 minutes.

CUSTARD:
COAGULATING PROTEIN

The process of changing liquid protein into a solid by heating it is called *coagulation*. Coagulation is a kind of denaturing. You used coagulated egg white to clarify stock in Chapter 3 (see pages 54–55). Egg white coagulates at about 156°F (69°C). It changes from an almost colorless, transparent, fairly thick liquid to a white solid. The protein in an egg yolk also coagulates when heated.

Protein coagulation is one of the main reasons the texture of food changes when it is cooked.

Meat and fish become firm, and batters change from liquids to solids. In fact, most baked goods have a "skeleton" of coagulated milk or egg protein that supports them.

Custard is a homogeneous mixture of eggs, milk, and sugar that has been heated to coagulate the protein in the eggs and the milk. The next experiment shows how different amounts of heat affect the coagulation of these proteins.

Materials & Equipment

+ ½ cup sugar
+ ⅛ teaspoon salt
+ 1 teaspoon vanilla
+ 2 cups milk
+ 3 eggs
+ measuring cups and spoons
+ a bowl
+ an electric mixer or eggbeater
+ 4 custard cups or other oven-proof cups
+ a pan the cups will fit into

Procedure

1 Preheat the oven to 325°F. Beat the sugar, salt, and vanilla into the milk. Add the eggs and beat well.

2 Divide the mixture equally among four custard cups. Set the cups in the pan and cover the bottom of the pan with about an inch of water.

(This is to make sure that the bottoms of the cups are not heated more than any other part.) Put the pan with the custards in the oven.

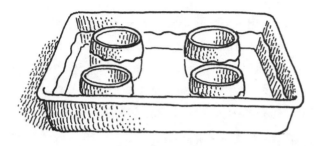

3 After 30 minutes, remove one cup of custard. Take the second cup out after 40 minutes, the third cup after 50 minutes, and the fourth cup after one hour.

Observations

Which custard has been properly cooked? Which custard has separated and has the most liquid?

When eggs first coagulate, the protein is able to trap and hold other liquids, such as the water in the milk and egg whites. If eggs are cooked too long or at too high a temperature, they become tougher and tougher and can no longer hold water. For example, scrambled eggs from which water has separated have been either overcooked or cooked too quickly.

Properly made custard is a smooth, shiny, yellow

pudding that slices cleanly when you put a spoon into it. There is no trace of water from either the egg or the milk.

All of these custards are good to eat. Refrigerate until you are ready to serve them. The overcooked custards should be drained before eating. They can be topped with fruit.

SOUR MILK BISCUITS: PROTEIN DENATURED BY ACID

Some protein is easily denatured by acid. You can tell when this happens if solid particles form in a liquid that contains dissolved protein, like milk. The protein in sour milk makes the milk thicker and ultimately separates from the watery portion of the milk. Certain bacteria make milk sour. Their acid waste products denature milk protein. But you can make a quick version of sour milk by adding your own acid.

Bring $\frac{1}{2}$ cup of milk to room temperature. Put 2 teaspoons of vinegar, a weak acid, in another cup. Pour the milk into the vinegar and stir. Let the mixture stand for about 10 minutes. How can you tell if the protein is denatured? Stir the milk. Can you get the denatured protein to dissolve?

You can use the sour milk to make biscuits. Just

substitute it for whole milk in a package of biscuit mix and follow the directions on the box, or make your own biscuits from scratch using this recipe.

Materials & Equipment

- ◆ I cup flour
- ◆ I teaspoon baking powder
- ◆ $\frac{1}{8}$ teaspoon baking soda
- ◆ $\frac{1}{2}$ teaspoon salt
- ◆ 2 tablespoons cold butter
- ◆ $\frac{1}{2}$ cup sour milk
- ◆ a medium-sized bowl
- ◆ a pastry blender or 2 knives
- ◆ a fork
- ◆ 2 spoons
- ◆ a cookie sheet

Procedure

1 Preheat the oven to 450°F. In a medium bowl, mix together the flour, baking powder, baking soda, and salt.

2 Using a pastry blender, or two knives, cut in the butter until the mixture looks like crumbs the size of small peas.

3 Add the sour milk and stir with a fork until all ingredients are thoroughly combined.

4 Drop the dough by spoonfuls onto the ungreased cookie sheet. Bake for 12–15 minutes until golden brown.

GELATIN:
SOL-GEL TRANSFORMATION

If all protein were as easily denatured as the soluble proteins in egg and milk, life could not survive. About 40 percent of the protein in our bodies and those of other animals is considerably tougher than egg and milk protein. It already exists as a solid that will not dissolve in water. This protein, called *collagen*, is found in cartilage, the white, flexible material at the ends of bones. It is also found in tendons, which attach muscles to bones, and ligaments, which tie bones together; and it is the main protein in bones themselves. Collagen is the protein that keeps us from falling apart.

As you might expect, collagen is also found in meat we eat. Tougher cuts of meat contain more collagen than more tender cuts. The problem facing cooks is how to make the collagen softer and meat more tender.

Fortunately, this is not a difficult task. When collagen is heated with water for a while, it breaks down into a smaller, softer, soluble protein called *gelatin*. The process of changing collagen to gelatin is speeded up with the addition of an acid like lemon juice, vinegar, or tomatoes to the cooking water. (Some cooks soak or marinate tough meats in vinegar before stewing.) A tomato stew should become tender sooner than one made in meat broth alone. Can you design an experiment to confirm this?

If you would like to prepare almost pure gelatin, get two or three veal bones from your butcher. Veal bones, which come from young calves, have a great deal of cartilage. (As animals grow older, cartilage is replaced with bone.) Cover the veal bones with water and boil for an hour. Strain the broth and let it cool. You can improve the taste of the gelatin in the broth by adding tomato juice.

Gelatin is different from collagen. Gelatin dissolves in hot water, while collagen doesn't dissolve at all. You can learn about some other properties of gelatin in the next experiment.

Materials & Equipment

+ ½ cup cold water

+ a package of unflavored gelatin

+ 1½ cups boiling water
+ a package of presweetened Kool-Aid
+ a measuring cup
+ a small bowl
+ a wooden spoon
+ a clear glass
+ a flashlight
+ a small pot
+ a 2-cup mold or 2-cup container
+ a plate

Procedure

1 Pour the cold water into a bowl and sprinkle the package of gelatin over it. Does the gelatin attract the water? How can you tell?

2 When the gelatin has been softened, add the boiling water and stir. Does the gelatin dissolve? This mixture is called a *sol*.

Taste the sol. Commercial gelatin is so tasteless that it can be used to make desserts as well as meat dishes.

3 Pour some of the sol into a clear glass. Shine a light through it. Does it show the Tyndall effect (see page 40)? What does this tell you about the size of gelatin molecules?

Let the sol cool in the glass, then chill it, uncovered. The most dramatic property of gelatin is revealed when a sol cools. It changes from a liquid to a semisolid quivering mass called a gel. Shine a light through the gel. Does it show the same Tyndall

effect as the sol? Is there any sign of water in the gel?

4 Put the gel in a pot and warm it over medium heat. Can you change the gel back into a sol by adding heat? Add $\frac{1}{2}$ package of presweetened Kool-Aid to the sol and stir with a wooden spoon until it is dissolved. Pour the flavored gelatin mixture into a mold, cool, and then chill until set.

5 Unmold the set gelatin by changing the gel next to the mold back into a sol. Fill the sink with hot water and have ready a plate that covers the top of the mold. Put the mold into the water for about 10 seconds. Be careful not to let

any water get on the gelatin. After removing the mold from the sink, put the plate over it, turn the

whole thing over, and give it a hard shake. You should hear the gelatin plop onto the plate. If the gelatin doesn't slip out, heat it again for a few seconds and repeat the procedure. Be careful that you don't heat it too much, as you can lose the sharp shape of the mold on your dessert.

A gelatin dessert can be unmolded long before it is to be served. Just return it to the refrigerator until you are ready to eat it.

Observations

The sol-gel transformation fascinated scientists. They wondered what happened to the water. Their research discovered that the water is trapped by a network of gelatin molecules that form when gelatin cools. They also discovered that as gelatin ages, it is able to hold less and less water.

See for yourself how gelatin loses moisture as it ages. Cut some of your gelatin dessert into 1-inch cubes. Leave the cubes, uncovered, on a plate in the refrigerator for several days. Every morning and evening, eat a cube to see how they begin to get tougher and tougher as they get dryer.

MUFFINS: A STUDY OF GLUTEN— THE WHEAT PROTEIN

Denatured protein is the "skeleton" that supports baked products. In cakes and muffins and other delicate baked goods, this support comes from coagulated milk and eggs. In bread, the support comes from a protein called *gluten* found in wheat flour.

Flour does not actually contain gluten. It contains two substances that can become gluten under the right conditions. The next experiment will show you some of the conditions needed to develop gluten and the effect of different amounts of gluten on the texture of muffins.

Materials & Equipment

- 1 cup all-purpose flour
- 2 tablespoons sugar
- 1 teaspoon salt
- 2 teaspoons baking powder
- 1 cup cake flour (not self-rising)
- 2 tablespoons butter
- ⅔ cup milk
- 2 eggs
- paper muffin-cup liners
- a 12-cup muffin tin
- measuring cups and spoons
- waxed paper
- a sifter
- 3 bowls
- a small frying pan

✦ an electric mixer
   or eggbeater

✦ 2 spoons

Procedure

1. Preheat the oven to 350°F. Put eight muffin-cup liners in the muffin tin, four on each side so you make two groups separated by four empty cups in the center. Use different-colored liners on each side or double line one side to help keep track of which cups hold which batter.

2. Sift about a cup of all-purpose flour onto a sheet of waxed paper. All-purpose flour contains more protein that can become gluten than cake flour. Measure out 1 cup of this flour and resift it along with 1 tablespoon of sugar, ½ teaspoon salt, and 1 teaspoon baking powder into a bowl.

3. Using a clean piece of waxed paper, repeat this process with cake flour instead of all-purpose flour. Cake flour has a lower potential gluten content. This mixture will be prepared in a way that keeps the gluten from developing.

4. Melt 1 tablespoon of butter in a frying pan and let it cool. In a clean bowl, beat ⅓ cup milk with 1 egg. Add the cooled butter and pour the mixture into the dry ingredients containing the all-purpose flour. Mix carefully until all the flour is moist, then beat the batter with an electric mixer

or eggbeater until it becomes smooth and glossy.

5 Repeat the steps for melting butter and mixing it with milk and egg. Add this second mixture all at once to the bowl with the cake flour. Stir quickly and lightly until all the flour is moist. You should not have to stir more than 15 seconds. Do not beat too hard and don't worry about lumps in the batter. How does this batter look compared with the other batter?

6 Spoon the batter containing cake flour into 4 muffin cups. Then spoon the all-purpose flour batter into the other 4 cups. Bake for 15 minutes until the tops are brown. Let the muffins cool.

Observations

Cut one of each kind of muffin in half. Which muffin has the finer grain? Which makes crumbs more easily? Taste the muffins. Which is more tender? Which has large tunnels caused by larger bubbles of gas?

Gluten develops when dough is warm and there is a lot of mixing. Gluten is prevented from developing when dough is kept cold and handled as little as possible. Some bread does not contain any protein other than gluten. Why do you think bread dough is kneaded? Why should pie dough be handled lightly and as little as possible?

There are many variations of this experiment.

Try making muffins with cake flour and with bread flour. Handle the batters the same way. See if temperature affects the way gluten develops. Use all-purpose flour but use ice-cold ingredients in one batter and room-temperature ingredients in the other. Which of the following baked products do you think depend on gluten for structure and which must be fairly gluten-free to remain flaky and tender—bread, cream puffs, pie crust, cake, biscuits? Can you think up experiments to test your ideas?

Kitchen Chemistry

The first chemists, called *alchemists*, were not searching for truth about nature or looking for a system to describe all matter. They worked long, hard hours over smelly cauldrons, which often contained dangerous materials, with a single idea to keep them going—finding a way to create gold. Nothing noble here. Just another get-rich-quick scheme.

You can't blame an alchemist for trying. Suppose you had plunged an iron pot into a perfectly ordinary-looking spring and found upon removing the pot some time later that it was covered with a red coating. You might reason, as they did, that if you could turn iron into something else, why not look

for a way to make gold from other metals? To this end, alchemists separated mixtures and mixed substances together. They developed many procedures used in laboratories today, and they discovered many substances no one knew existed.

But the alchemists failed in their intended purpose. No matter how hard they tried, they could not make gold. Nothing personal here. The alchemists didn't know that no one can make gold, for gold is an element—a substance that cannot be broken down. But alchemists did make many other important discoveries. Perhaps the most important were the events they observed in which one kind of matter did change into another. These events are *chemical reactions.*

There are hundreds of thousands of different chemical reactions. The flame from a gas burner, the rust on an old piece of iron, and the browning of a cut apple are three examples. Despite the obvious differences, all chemical reactions have certain things in common.

In every chemical reaction, you start with one kind of matter and end up with another. Often the products of a reaction have very different properties from the reactants you began with. For example, when propane gas in a stove reacts with oxygen in the air, the products are carbon dioxide

and water vapor. This reaction can be written as a chemical equation:

$$propane\ gas + oxygen + starter\ heat \rightarrow$$
$$carbon\ dioxide + water + flame$$

All chemical reactions involve energy, which may be in the form of heat, light, or electricity. Chemists usually find heat is the easiest way to measure energy involved in reactions. All chemical reactions can be divided into one of two kinds: those that give off heat and those that take up heat. Some reactions, like burning, need a small amount of heat to get started but give off energy once they get going.

Many times a chemical reaction is not as obvious as the flame of a gas burner. There are other ways of knowing when a chemical reaction has taken place. In this chapter, you will learn some of these ways and how chemical reactions play a significant part in the preparation of food.

LEMON FIZZ:
A REACTION FORMS A GAS

Sometimes a gas is the product of a chemical reaction. If the reaction takes place in a solution, bubbles rise to the surface and are easy to see.

Materials & Equipment

+ water
+ I teaspoon baking soda
+ lemonade

+ measuring spoons
+ 2 glass tumblers
+ 2 spoons

Procedure

I Fill one glass half full of water. Add ½ teaspoon of baking soda and stir with one of your spoons. Does the baking soda dissolve easily? Is there any reaction? Use red-cabbage indicator (see Chapter 2, pages 25–26) to test this solution to see if it is an acid or a base. Pour a little of the solution into a small amount of the indicator.

2 Fill the second glass half full of lemonade. (Test the lemonade with the indicator in another container.) Using a clean spoon stir ½ teaspoon of baking soda into the lemonade. How can you tell that there was a reaction? Drink the lemon fizz quickly before all the bubbles escape into the air.

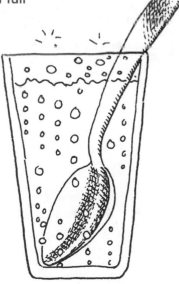

Observations

Invent other experiments to see if baking soda reacts with other acid drinks. Try making orange fizz or apple fizz.

Baking soda is a compound of sodium, carbon, hydrogen, and oxygen. It reacts with acids to give off carbon dioxide.

CUPCAKES: HOW CAKES RISE

The changes that occur as a cake bakes are very dramatic. As the batter gets warmer, tiny bubbles of gas form in the mixture and grow larger. The batter surrounding these bubbles becomes permanently set as the protein from milk and eggs coagulates with heat. Flour strengthens the walls of these bubbles so the cake doesn't collapse when removed from the oven. Sugar and flour hold moisture to make a tender crumb. The ingredients play an important part in the structure of a cake. Perhaps the most remarkable thing about this amazing structure is that it is delicious to eat.

Since the source of the lightness and delicacy of a cake is gas bubbles, it's fun to investigate the bubble-

producing reactions. Then we'll investigate how bubbles help make a cake rise.

Materials & Equipment

+ ½ teaspoon cream of tartar
+ water
+ ½ teaspoon baking soda
+ 1½ teaspoons double-acting

baking powder
+ measuring spoons
+ 4 glass tumblers
+ 4 spoons
+ a small saucepan
+ a candy thermometer

Procedure 1

1 Put about ½ teaspoon of cream of tartar in half a glass of cold water. Stir to dissolve. Is there any reaction? Test a small amount of the solution with red cabbage indicator. Is it acid or base?

2 Add about ½ teaspoon of baking soda to the cream of tartar solution. Be sure to wipe off your measuring spoon before you dip it into the baking soda box and use a clean spoon to stir the mixture.

Observations

Is there any reaction? What gas is released? How would your findings from lemon fizz predict this result?

There used to be a baking-powder product made with cream of tartar (also known as tartaric acid), baking soda, and cornstarch. Cream of tartar is an acid that can be packaged in a dry form and dissolves quickly in liquid. The cornstarch absorbs moisture in the powder mixture, so that the baking soda and cream of tartar are prevented from reacting with each other in the box. Batter mixed with cream of tartar baking powder had to be baked as soon as it was mixed. If it stood around for a while before baking, most of the gas escaped and the cake did not rise as much. You can test this idea with the cupcake recipe and some experimental procedures given in the next section.

Procedure 2

1 Half fill one glass with cold water and a second glass with hot water. Add $1/2$ teaspoon of double-acting baking powder to each glass. In which glass is the reaction stronger?

2 When no more bubbles are coming out in the first glass, heat the solution in a pan. Is there a second reaction?

Observations

A second type of baking powder was developed that could stand around and wait in batter before being baked. It contained an acid called sodium aluminum sulfate, which reacted with baking soda only when heated. So the carbon dioxide would be produced only when the cake was being baked.

There were two problems with baking powder containing sodium aluminum sulfate. First, it left a bitter aftertaste in the cake. Secondly, for certain recipes, the heat of the oven might set the structure of the cake before any gas was released, forming a very heavy product. For this reason, double-acting baking powder was developed. It contains two acid powders: a quick-acting acid powder, like cream of tartar, that starts releasing carbon dioxide as soon as it is mixed with a liquid, and sodium aluminum sulfate, to release more carbon dioxide when it is baked. Less of this acid is needed in such a powder, so there is less bitter aftertaste.

Procedure 3

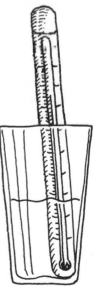

1 Heat water until it is about 150°F (66°C). (Use a candy thermometer to measure temperature.) Half fill a glass tumbler with the hot water. Put the candy thermometer in the water.

2 When the temperature reading levels off and stays the same for

about five seconds, add a heaping teaspoonful of double-acting baking powder and stir.

Observations

Watch the thermometer as the reaction takes place. Does the solution get warmer or colder? By how many degrees? You can repeat this experiment using different amounts of baking powder.

What you have just witnessed is an example of a chemical reaction that takes up heat. Unlike combustion, in which heat is given off, the chemical reaction in which sodium aluminum sulfate breaks down and releases carbon dioxide requires heat to begin. The heat for this reaction is removed from the surrounding liquid, making it cooler.

Use the cupcake recipe below in the following experiments, which reveal how different baking powders act in batter.

Basic Cupcake Recipe

Materials & Equipment

- ✦ 1 cup cake flour (not self-rising)
- ✦ $\frac{1}{2}$ cup sugar
- ✦ $\frac{1}{4}$ teaspoon salt
- ✦ 1 egg

- ✦ 1 teaspoon double-acting baking powder

- ✦ ¼ cup butter (½ stick), softened
- ✦ ¼ cup milk
- ✦ 1 teaspoon vanilla
- ✦ measuring cups and spoons
- ✦ waxed paper
- ✦ sifter
- ✦ two mixing bowls
- ✦ electric mixer
- ✦ spoon
- ✦ 12-cup muffin tin, greased or with paper liners

Basic Procedure

1 Preheat the oven to 350°F. Sift onto waxed paper and then measure the flour. Resift with the sugar, salt, and baking powder (or baking powder substitute, depending on the experiment) into a bowl. Set dry ingredients aside.

2 In a separate bowl, beat the softened butter with an electric mixer. Next beat in the egg, milk, and vanilla.

3 Add the liquid ingredients all at once to the dry ingredients. Stir carefully until all the flour is moistened, then beat just until the batter is smooth.

4 Pour the batter into 4 muffin cups. Bake for about 15 minutes. The cupcakes are done when the tops are brown and a toothpick stuck into a cupcake comes out clean.

Variation 1

Make 2 batches of cupcakes substituting $\frac{1}{2}$ teaspoon of baking soda and $\frac{1}{4}$ teaspoon of cream of tartar for the baking powder in each. Mix up the first batch and let it stand in its mixing bowl for at least an hour before you mix the second batch. Bake both batches at the same time.

Variation 2

Try making the cupcakes with different amounts of baking powder. Use $\frac{1}{2}$ teaspoon for one batch, 1 teaspoon for a second batch, and $1\frac{1}{2}$ teaspoons for a third batch.

Variation 3

If you want to try one large experiment, first mix a batter using $\frac{1}{2}$ teaspoon cream of tartar and $\frac{1}{4}$ teaspoon baking soda instead of the baking powder. Let this batter stand for about a half hour and then mix 2 more batters. In the second batch use the double-acting baking powder called for in the recipe. Then make a third batch the same as the first, using cream of tartar and baking soda. Bake all 3 batches together in a muffin tin with 12 cups. Since each batch makes 4 cupcakes, you can use one muffin tin for the entire experiment.

When you compare cupcakes, look for differences in height, crumb size, and taste.

Note: It's fun to watch a cake bake. If you have an oven with a window, leave the light on and look in during the baking process. If you don't have such a window, don't open the oven before it is time for the cupcakes to be done. If a blast of cold air hits a cake before it is finished setting, the hot gas in the cake suddenly contracts and the cake falls. Since the centers set last, a draft often produces a cake with a fallen center.

CARAMEL SYRUP: SUGAR DECOMPOSES

Some compounds, like sugar, break down into simpler compounds and elements when heated. Sugar melts at 320°F (160°C) and starts to break down or decompose at 356°F (180°C). When sugar breaks down, water is one product and carbon is another. As more and more carbon forms, the liquid sugar becomes straw colored and eventually turns a dark brown. Sugar that has been partly broken down is known as caramel.

You can see the chemical breakdown of sugar when you make caramel. Be very careful in following

the directions for this experiment, because you will be working with very hot material. You should have an adult help you with this experiment.

Materials & Equipment

+ ½ cup sugar
+ ½ cup water

+ a small, heavy frying pan
+ a wooden spoon

Procedure

1 Put the sugar in a small, heavy frying pan. Stirring constantly, cook the sugar over medium heat. It will soon melt and start turning brown. When the sugar is straw colored, remove the pan from the heat.

2 *Slowly and carefully* add the water. The caramel will be brittle and very hot. If you add water too quickly, it may spatter and burn you.

3 Return the pan to low heat and stir for about 10 minutes. Try to get all the caramel to dissolve. After 10 minutes, remove the pan from the heat and let the syrup cool.

Observations

When the syrup has cooled completely, taste it and compare the taste to sugar. Which is sweeter? You can serve this syrup over ice cream or use it to glaze the cupcakes from the last experiment.

For a second experiment, try heating $1/2$ cup sugar until it is dark brown. Again, turn off the heat and add about $1/2$ cup water. This time you will have to be even more careful, as the caramel is so hot there may be a violent reaction. A solution made of dark caramel is used to color gravies and stews. The sugar has been broken down so completely that no sweetness remains.

What change in the appearance of the sugar let you know that a chemical reaction was taking place? Can you think of any other color changes that are the result of a chemical reaction?

VITAMIN C FRUIT SALAD: OXIDATION OF FRUIT

Ever notice how certain fruits and vegetables turn brown when a cut surface is exposed to the air? This happens because there is a pigment in fruit that reacts with the oxygen in air (more on this

reaction in Chapter 10). Oxygen is a very reactive element, which combines with many substances in a reaction called, fittingly, *oxidation*. Oxidation is a chemical reaction that always gives off energy. Combustion is oxidation of a fuel that is so rapid that a flame is produced. Rusting iron is slower oxidation that produces heat (but not so that you'd notice it under ordinary conditions). When an apple turns brown, oxidation is also fairly slow.

Apples, peaches, pears, and bananas are all easily oxidized. A fresh fruit salad can be protected from oxidation, however, by keeping it from the air or by treating it with vitamin C. Do the next experiment and see how.

Materials & Equipment

- ✦ water
- ✦ 1 chewable vitamin C tablet
- ✦ 1 apple
- ✦ 1 peach or 1 pear
- ✦ 1 banana
- ✦ a small deep bowl
- ✦ a sharp knife
- ✦ a slotted spoon
- ✦ 2 shallow soup bowls

Procedure

1 Put about a cup of water in the small, deep bowl and dissolve the vitamin C tablet in it.

2 Cut the apple in half. Peel and cut out the core of one half quickly. Slice this half into the bowl

of vitamin C solution. Make sure each slice is covered with the solution. Remove the apple slices with a slotted spoon and put them in one of the shallow bowls.

3 Peel, core, and then slice the other half of the apple directly into the other shallow bowl.

4 Repeat this procedure with the other fruits: Slice half into the vitamin C solution and leave slices from the other half untreated. Put all the vitamin C pieces in one bowl and the untreated pieces in the other. Arrange the fruit so that as much surface is exposed to the air as possible.

Let the two fruit salads stand for an hour or more. Watch to see where browning occurs.

Observations

Can you see a difference between the treated and untreated fruit? Why do you think lemon juice is

put on apple slices as they are being prepared for apple pie? Do lemons contain vitamin C? Other fruits and vegetables that brown when exposed to air are eggplants, avocados, and raw potatoes. Can you design an experiment to see if vitamin C slows down their oxidation?

Oxidation of fruit is affected by temperature. You can test this by making two fruit salads. Leave one at room temperature and put the other in the refrigerator. Which salad browns first?

The term *oxidation* is used by chemists for any re-action in which substances combine in a manner similar to the way they combine with oxygen. The oxidation reaction of these fruits is sped up be-cause of a certain protein in the fruit known as an *enzyme* (more on enzymes in Chapter 10). Before the fruit is cut, the enzyme and the compounds that will turn brown in the presence of oxygen are sepa-rated from each other. But when cells are injured as the fruit is cut, the enzyme and the compounds come in contact with each other and oxidation oc-curs. The enzyme is not present in melons and cit-rus fruits. They will eventually turn brown in air, but without the enzyme it takes days instead of min-utes.

Fruits that oxidize easily will also react with cop-per and iron. Put a fruit salad in a copper bowl or

an iron pan. Compare the browning of that salad with a fruit salad in a glass or china bowl. Cover these salads with plastic wrap to reduce oxidation with the air.

All the fruit salads in these experiments are good to eat, even if the fruit is discolored. Combine all the fruit when you have finished experimenting. Add a small can of apricots or some fruit syrup and chill before serving.

FRUIT AND TEA PUNCH: TESTING FOR IRON

For most people a test tube symbolizes chemistry. The beauty of the test tube is that it allows the chemist to combine small amounts of material in a vessel where it is easy to see if a chemical reaction takes place.

There are several changes that let you know when a reaction is taking place. In the experiments you have done up to now, you've seen reactions that produce a gas and reactions that produce a color change. Another way is to see a clear solution become cloudy as solid particles form. Such solid particles are called *precipitates*. You will be looking for a precipitate in the next experiment.

If you have a chemistry set with test tubes, use them for this experiment. If you don't, use small, clear, colorless juice glasses.

There are certain chemicals in tea that react with iron compounds in fruit juices to form a precipitate. This precipitate is very annoying if you are preparing a punch made with tea. All too often a crystal-clear iced tea punch becomes cloudy. Although the punch may taste fine, its muddy look is not what the party giver had in mind. Not all fruits contain iron, however. Learn which ones do in the next experiment and keep your iced tea punch sparkling clear.

Materials & Equipment

+ 2 cups of strong tea
+ an assortment of fruit juices, including canned and bottled juices, red juices, pineapple juice, and prune juice
+ juice glasses or test tubes
+ pen and paper

Procedure

1 Set out a row of small glasses or test tubes and put about an inch of tea in each glass. Label the glasses for each juice you are going to test.

2 You might also want to prepare a data sheet to record your observations. Here is an example of what a data sheet might look like:

FRUIT JUICE	TEST RESULT
orange	–
canned pineapple	–
cranberry	?
cherry Hi-C	?

3 Add about an inch of juice to each glass of tea. Watch for cloudiness. If a precipitate forms, put a plus sign (+) next to the name of the juice on your data sheet. If no precipitate forms and the mixture remains clear, put a minus sign (–). If you are not certain, put a ? on the data sheet and test the juice again. Some juices are cloudy to begin with. Make sure that a new precipitate forms by comparing the tea mixture with a plain sample of juice.

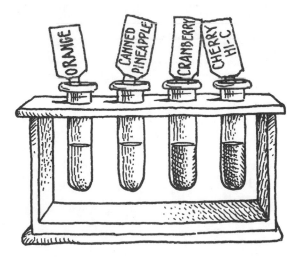

Observations

Which juices contain iron? Do canned juices contain more iron than bottled juices? According to a table of food composition, which tells the various vitamins, minerals, fats, proteins, etc., in food, the juices that contain the most iron are red juices, pineapple juice, and prune juice. Do your findings agree with this?

When you have finished the experiment, pour all the mixtures into a pitcher. Taste it to see if you might like to add more of any particular juice. Add any leftover tea. Pour over ice to serve.

Plants We Eat

All living things need a constant supply of energy in order to stay alive. The source of this energy is food combining with oxygen. The oxidation of food (sugar is an example) is the same basic overall reaction as that of fuel combining with oxygen to produce a fire. (There is, of course, a big difference that I'll tell you about in a minute.) Here's an equation that shows the similarity between the reactions:

$$\text{sugar (fuel) + oxygen} \rightarrow$$
$$\text{carbon dioxide + water + energy (fire)}$$

When a fuel burns, the released energy is rapid and uncontrolled. In living things, there are many steps in the oxidation of food and the energy is released in a carefully controlled manner so that it can be used for the various activities of living. Scientists can measure the amount of energy that can be released from different kinds of food as heat energy. They put weighed amounts of food in a special instrument called a calorimeter. The food is burned with oxygen, and the heat energy given off by the reaction raises the temperature of the water outside the chamber where the food is burning. The change in temperature of the water is a measure of the amount of energy in the food. This heat is measured in calories. If you look in most general cookbooks, you can find a table that lists the calories in different foods. Fats have the most calories and proteins have the least.

We use the energy we get from food for moving and thinking and responding to the world. Energy from food goes into building new molecules of protein and carbohydrates in our bodies. Any leftover energy not used for these activities is used to build fat molecules.

The average growing kid needs between 2,600 and 3,000 calories a day. If you eat more than this and don't do enough to use them up, you will gain weight.

As one organism feeds on another, energy is passed along, forming a food chain linking all forms of life to each other. Meat eaters feed on plant eaters, some microorganisms feed on dead or living organisms, and plant eaters feed on plants. The question is: What organisms are at the bottom of the food chain? These living things must be able to get energy from some source other than feeding on other living things, and they must be able to convert this energy into a substance that is food for themselves. On our planet, the bottom of the food chain is plants.

Green plants produce their own food through a chemical reaction that is the reverse of the reaction in our bodies when we oxidize sugar:

carbon dioxide + water + energy →

sugar + oxygen

The outside source of energy for this reaction is sunlight. Carbon dioxide is present in air, and water is present in soil. The green pigment *chlorophyll* gives plants the ability to make sugar with these raw materials. This process of food manufacturing is called *photosynthesis*, which means "putting together with light."

Plants use the sugar made during photosynthesis to make proteins, other carbohydrates, and oils.

So when animals eat plants they get energy that originally came from the sun. The importance of green plants to all other forms of life on earth is clear. Without them, we could not survive.

The experiments in this chapter will show you some of the activities of plants that help keep them alive.

RAW VEGETABLE SALAD: HOW PLANTS TAKE IN WATER

The roots of a plant have several jobs. Most roots anchor a plant to the ground. Some roots, such as carrots, also store food made in the leaves. But their most important job is to absorb water from the soil.

Look at the tip of a fresh carrot that has not been trimmed or packaged. The main root becomes very slender at the tip, and there are many small roots sticking out from it. Look at these smaller roots with a magnifying glass. There are many tiny branches off each rootlet that increase the surface area of the root so more water can be absorbed. If you can't get an untrimmed carrot, put a fresh carrot, tip down, in a glass of water. It will develop new rootlets in a few days.

Water is absorbed into roots by a process called *osmosis*. In osmosis, water passes through a thin sheet of living material called a *cell membrane*. Cell membranes have holes in them that are larger than water molecules.

If the holes in cell membranes are bigger than water molecules, how come water flows *into* roots when it could just as easily flow *out!* Do the next experiment and discover the answer.

Materials & Equipment

+ a large carrot
+ water
+ salt

+ a vegetable peeler
+ 2 bowls
+ 2 spoons

Procedure

1 Peel the carrot. (Be sure to move the peeler away from your fingers.) Use the peeler to make strips of carrot.

2 Divide the strips between two bowls and add enough water to each bowl to completely

cover the strips. Put about a tablespoon of salt into one of the bowls and stir. The water should taste very salty.

3 Let the carrots soak for several hours. From time to time, take a strip from each bowl and bend it and taste it to see how crisp it is.

Observations

Which carrots are crisper? Which carrots have absorbed water and which have lost water?

The direction water flows in roots depends on the minerals dissolved in the water. When more minerals are inside the roots than in soil water, water flows into the roots, making them firm and crisp. When there are more minerals in the soil water than in roots' cells, water flows *out* of the roots, making them wilted and soft.

You can do many variations of this experiment with other vegetables. Thin slices of cucumber work especially well. Try different amounts of salt to see how fast wilting occurs. Find out if wilting occurs more quickly in warm (not hot) water than in cold water.

You can make a salad with all the vegetables from this experiment. Chill, then drain, the vegetables. Make a dressing of sour cream and fresh chopped dill or parsley, or try the vinaigrette from Chapter 3 (see pages 41–42).

STRIPED CELERY SNACK: HOW WATER MOVES UP STEMS

One of the important jobs of plant stems is to carry water from the roots to the leaves. You can see how this happens with a stalk of celery and some food coloring.

Materials & Equipment

- celery stalks
- water
- food coloring
- 2 glasses
- vegetable peeler
- a knife
- a plastic sandwich bag

Procedure 1

1. Put a stalk of celery in half a glass of water colored with several drops of red food coloring.

2. When the water has moved all the way up the stem, use a vegetable peeler to shave away the outer surface of the celery.

Observations

Which parts of the stem have the most food coloring? The long strands that carry water are called the *xylem*. Xylem is made of hollow cells that form a

xylem

pipeline from roots to leaves. You can see where the xylem is in celery by cutting across the stalk.

Procedure 2

| Repeat this experiment using 2 stalks of celery. One stalk should be quite leafy and the other should have no leaves.

Observations

In which stalk does the water reach the top of the stem first?

Procedure 3

| For this experiment use two leafy stalks of celery. Put one glass with its celery stalk in the sunlight and keep the other in the shade, covering the celery with a small plastic bag.

Observations

In which stalk does the water rise more quickly? How do your findings support the theory that the speed with which water rises in plants is a result of how fast water evaporates from the leaves?

You can eat the celery when you have finished your experiments. It's good with some peanut butter or cream cheese spread down the middle.

Try putting other vegetables in colored water. See if you can find the xylem in white radishes, scal-

lions, and carrots. Choose a dark-colored dye that will show up against the color of the vegetables.

SPINACH: COLOR CHANGES IN CHLOROPHYLL

Spinach is a treat for many food lovers. But if you don't love spinach, perhaps it's because it was over-cooked when you had it. When overcooked, spinach is a limp, unappetizing gray-green.

Fresh spinach, on the other hand, is a beautiful, rich green. When it is first put in boiling water, this green brightens as gases in the cells are forced out by heating. After this, the spinach becomes grayer and grayer. Cooking releases certain acids in spinach that change the color of chlorophyll.

The amount of acid that is released during cooking is very small. It would be possible to keep spinach a bright green if this acid could be removed as soon as it was released into the cooking water. A pinch of baking soda added to the cooking water will react with the acid and "neutralize" it. (Try this to see if it works.) Baking soda, however, makes vegetables mushy, so it is not often used.

When chemists want to prevent a solution from becoming too acid or basic, they use another kind of solution called a *buffer*. Buffers can absorb any

acid or basic molecules and take them out of a solution as soon as they are released into it. Of course, many buffers used in laboratories are not suitable for eating. But one substance we do eat that can act as a buffer is milk.

Is it possible to preserve the color of spinach by cooking it in milk? Do the next experiment to find out.

Materials & Equipment

- ✦ milk
- ✦ water
- ✦ several fresh, washed spinach leaves
- ✦ a measuring cup
- ✦ 2 saucepans
- ✦ a slotted spoon
- ✦ a white plate

Procedure

1 Put 1 cup of milk in 1 saucepan and 1 cup of water in the other. Warm the liquids over low heat.

2 When they begin to simmer, drop a few leaves of spinach into each pan. Keep the temperature low so that the milk simmers but doesn't boil. Cook the spinach for 4 or 5 minutes. Turn off the heat and let the spinach stay in the hot liquids for another few minutes.

3 Remove the spinach with a slotted spoon to a white plate and compare the colors of the

cooked spinach leaves to each other and to a raw spinach leaf.

Observations

Have the colors changed after cooking? Which seems grayer, the spinach cooked in water or the spinach cooked in milk?

Choose either milk or water to cook the rest of the spinach. Season with salt, pepper, and butter to serve.

BOILED WINTER SQUASH: A STUDY OF CELLULOSE

The experiment you did to show how water gets into plants also showed how water is important for support. Without water, plants become wilted and limp. But in addition to water, plants contain a carbohydrate called *cellulose* that plays an important role in the supporting structure of a plant.

The soft protoplasm of each plant cell is surrounded on all sides by a cell wall made up mainly of cellulose. Cellulose is firmer than protoplasm, and the cell walls help to support a plant against the force of gravity.

Like starches, cellulose is made of chains of sugar

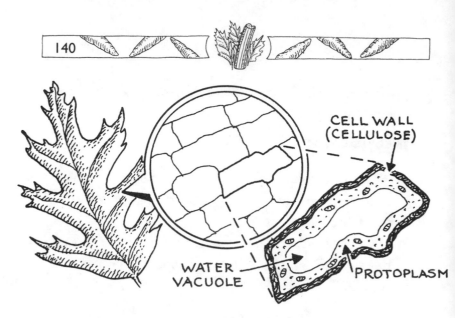

CELL WALL (CELLULOSE)

WATER VACUOLE

PROTOPLASM

molecules linked together. Cellulose would be a good source of food for us if we could digest it but, unfortunately, we can't. The sugar molecules in cellulose are linked together differently than the molecules in starch. Cellulose links make the chain rigid and make it useless to us as food, because our digestive tracts have no way of breaking these links. Some animals, like cows, have microorganisms in their stomachs that can break down the links in a cellulose chain. For this reason, they can live on hay and grass. But the cellulose in plants we eat leaves our bodies pretty much as it entered. It does, however, serve a useful function as fiber—also called roughage—which stimulates our digestive tracts.

The main reason we cook vegetables is to soften the cellulose so that it passes through our bodies more easily. The next experiment shows some of

the conditions that change the rate at which cellulose softens during cooking.

Materials & Equipment

- ✦ a small butternut or other hard winter squash
- ✦ water
- ✦ I teaspoon vinegar
- ✦ ½ teaspoon baking soda
- ✦ a vegetable peeler
- ✦ a large, sharp knife

- ✦ cutting board
- ✦ a spoon
- ✦ 3 saucepans
- ✦ measuring spoons
- ✦ a slotted spoon
- ✦ a fork
- ✦ a potato masher or electric mixer

Procedure

1 Peel the squash with the vegetable peeler, then cut it in half the long way. Be prepared; it will be hard to cut. Scrape out the seeds and pith with a spoon. Cut the squash into one-inch cubes, trying to keep them a similar size.

2 Divide the squash between 3 saucepans and add enough water to each to cover the squash. Add I teaspoon of vinegar to one pan and ½ teaspoon of baking soda to another. The third pan containing only water is a control.

3 Cook all 3 pans over medium heat. Bring each pan to a boil and let it continue boiling while you make your observations.

4 Every few minutes remove a piece of squash from each pan with a slotted spoon. Test it for softness by trying to mash it with a fork.

Observations

Which squash becomes soft first? Does cooking squash in acid speed up the rate of softening cellulose?

When all the squash is cooked, drain it and then mash it with a potato masher or an electric mixer. The squash is good plain, but even better if you add 2 tablespoons butter, 2 tablespoons of brown sugar, and a dash of salt and pepper.

As you might expect, the length of cooking time for vegetables depends on the amount of cellulose in the plant. Leafy vegetables, such as spinach, do not contain much cellulose and need only be cooked a few minutes. Artichokes, on the other hand, are high in cellulose and must be cooked quite a while to get soft. Design an experiment to check this out.

CHOP SUEY:
HOW BEANS SPROUT

One of the main sources of food for people is seeds. Cereal grains, corn, rice, and beans are all

seeds. Every seed is a remarkable package. It appears to be very simple. Yet it contains the cells that will become a plant and all the food needed for the baby plant to get a good start. Seeds are able to go through long periods of dryness and extreme cold and still burst with new life when conditions are right.

You can easily create the right conditions for sprouting seeds.

Materials & Equipment

+ ¹/₄ cup dried beans such as lentils, limas, kidneys, or blackeyes
+ water
+ a bowl
+ a colander
+ a clean, unglazed pot (a new flowerpot is good)
+ a saucer to cover the pot

Procedure

1 Put the beans in the bowl and cover with water. Let them soak overnight. The starch in the beans absorbs the water and the beans will swell.

2 The next day, moisten the inside of a new flowerpot with water. Drain the beans in a colander and put them in the flowerpot. In order for

beans to sprout, they must be kept moist but not wet. Cover the pot with the saucer and put it in a closet.

3 Check the beans every day. If they appear dry or develop the smell of fermenting beans, wash them by running water over them in a colander and drain them well. Rinse out the flowerpot before you return the beans to it.

Observations

The first structure to grow from a seed is the root. This anchors the seedling to the ground and makes sure that there will be a continuous supply of water for the growing plant. Beans have two seedling leaves that contain stored food. (Do these contain chlorophyll when they first emerge?) When beans sprout in soil, these thick leaves are pushed up through the soil and become green. They make food until the thinner foliage leaves develop and take over the job. Then the seed leaves shrivel and die.

Additional Procedures

There are many experiments you can do to see how different conditions affect the sprouting of seeds. Put some soaked seeds in the refrigerator and compare them with seeds sprouting at room

temperature. Find out if light and darkness affect sprouting. Take a few seeds just when the roots appear and put them between two pieces of moist folded paper towels held together by paper clips. Keep the towels moist and prop them up so the roots are pointed upward, away from the pull of gravity. Watch to see how these roots grow after several days.

Add the sprouts to canned or frozen chop suey and heat just until hot. They should be crisp and delicious.

POPCORN:
MEASURING MOISTURE IN SEEDS

No matter how dry seeds seem to be, all seeds contain a tiny bit of water that keeps the cells alive until conditions are favorable for sprouting. It is this tiny bit of water that makes popcorn popable.

When a kernel of popping corn is heated quickly, the water inside the kernel becomes a gas that exerts pressure strong enough to burst the tough seed coat. Once free of its container, the gas expands rapidly, causing the soft starch in the seed to puff up into millions of tiny rigid-walled bubbles.

What happens to the popability of popcorn

when you change the amount of moisture in the seed? Do the next experiment to find out.

Materials & Equipment

- ✦ fresh popping corn
- ✦ water
- ✦ 9 tablespoons vegetable oil
- ✦ measuring cups and spoons
- ✦ a cookie sheet
- ✦ a jar with a cover
- ✦ a hot air popper or a deep pot with a lid
- ✦ 3 identical 8-ounce glass tumblers
- ✦ a ruler

Procedure

1.

2. MOISTURE

3. MOISTURE/GAS EXPANDING DUE TO HEAT

4.

1 Preheat the oven to 200°F. Put ½ cup of popping corn in a single layer on a cookie sheet and bake for 2 hours. (Does any corn pop during the heating? If not, why not?)

2 Put another ½ cup of popping corn in a jar. Add 1 tablespoon of water. Put the cover on the jar and shake it so that the water coats all the seeds. Let the jar stand overnight. Every few hours, give the jar a shake to redistribute the water. (You can let it stand without shaking while you sleep.)

3 The next day pop the ½ cup of dried corn, the ½ cup of wet corn, and ½ cup of untreated corn in 3 separate batches. A hot-air popper works best, but if you don't have a popper, you can use a deep pot with a cover. Put about 3 tablespoons of vegetable oil on the bottom of the pot and add 2 kernels of popcorn from one batch. Heat the oil over high heat until the 2 kernels pop. Then add the rest of that batch of corn, cover, and shake over lower heat until popping stops. Remove the popcorn from the heat. Repeat for the other two batches.

4 Count 50 popped kernels from the first group into a glass and measure how high the popcorn reaches. This is a measure of the volume of the popped corn. Measure 50 popped kernals from the other 2 batches in the same way and compare. Which corn has the largest volume? Which has the smallest?

Observations

How does the volume of the heated corn compare to the volume of the moistened corn and the untreated corn? The amount of moisture in popcorn is crucial to the size of the finished product. Popcorn manufacturers make it their business to know just how much water is needed. Popcorn is harvested

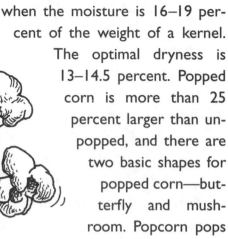

when the moisture is 16–19 percent of the weight of a kernel. The optimal dryness is 13–14.5 percent. Popped corn is more than 25 percent larger than unpopped, and there are two basic shapes for popped corn—butterfly and mushroom. Popcorn pops when inside steam reaches 347°F (175°C) and the pressure is 9 times atmospheric pressure or 135 pounds per square inch. At this point the seed coat ruptures, and the internal starch rapidly expands into bubbles that solidify as they cool.

There are other seeds you can try to pop. Compare expensive popcorn with inexpensive brands. Try popping sweet corn seeds. Put a little oil in the bottom of a deep pot with a cover. Shake the seeds as you heat them. When I popped sweet corn, I got corn nuts. Another seed that pops is amaranth grain, which you can buy at health food stores. Pop them in a pot without oil. Use a magnifying glass to examine the popped amaranth.

Microwave popcorn also lends itself to some experiments . . . coming up in the next chapter.

CHAPTER 8

Microwave Cooking

There are thousands of professional food scientists who make a living working on science experiments you can eat. One of the biggest challenges to these scientists since this book was first published is the microwave oven.

Microwaves are a form of energy that occur in nature in sunlight as well as in the light from all other stars. Microwaves are one kind of *electromagnetic radiation*. Others are visible light, radio waves, X rays, gamma rays, and cosmic rays.

When microwaves come into contact with water molecules, they make the molecules twist their position. Microwave ovens produce a high concentration of microwave radiation, alternating its direction

back and forth between 915 and 2,450 million times per second. Water molecules bombarded by microwaves twist back and forth that many times. They move! Increased motion of water molecules becomes heat energy that can cook food. Since the microwaves act directly on the water in food, and not on the container or the air in the oven, the food heats up while the oven itself stays cool. Cooking containers get hot as heat is transferred from the food to the container.

Microwaves in an oven are generated by a device called a *magnetron*, which uses a magnet to make electrons travel rapidly in a circular path. The circling electrons generate microwaves that pass through a wave guide to the top of the oven, where

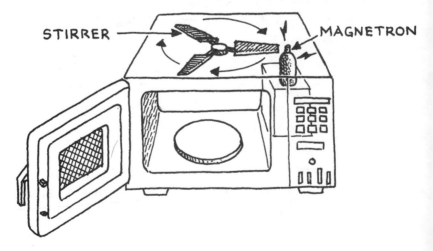

STIRRER — MAGNETRON

the waves strike a rotating "stirrer" that looks something like a propeller. As the microwaves reflect off the stirrer, they are distributed in all directions into the space of the oven. The waves also bounce off the oven walls. Ideally, the microwaves should be evenly distributed throughout the oven so that food cooks evenly. But in reality, even with stirrers, all microwave ovens have hot spots. Putting food on a rotating carousel is one way to make sure it cooks evenly. You can make a map of the hot spots in your microwave oven with the next experiment.

HONEY CAKE:
A MAP OF MICROWAVE HOT SPOTS

A mixture of honey and flour will caramelize to show the places where the microwaves are focused.

Materials & Equipment

- ✦ 1 cup cake flour
- ✦ 1 teaspoon baking soda
- ✦ 1 egg
- ✦ 1 cup honey
- ✦ measuring cups and spoons
- ✦ mixing bowl
- ✦ a big spoon
- ✦ 9" x 13" glass baking dish

Procedure 1

1 Measure the flour and baking soda into the bowl. Stir in the egg, then the honey to make a smooth mixture.

2 Pour the batter into the baking dish and smooth out the surface so that there is a thin layer that completely covers the bottom.

3 If your microwave has a revolving tray, remove it and then microwave on high for 7 minutes.

Observations

Notice the pattern of browning on the top of the cake. This shows where the microwaves are focused in the oven to form hotter areas. The brownness is due to the caramelizing of the honey. Is the browning on top only, or does it go through the thickness of the cake? What does the browning tell you about the way the inside of the cake is heated compared to the outside? If your microwave has a revolving tray, try cooking another honey cake using the tray. How effective is this

method for counteracting the hot spots in your oven?

I cannot recommend this cake for its taste. Microwaving seems to develop the gluten in wheat flour, and it also causes a gummy material to form on the bottom of the cake. You might want to experiment to see if you can improve the recipe by adding butter and substituting another kind of flour for the wheat flour.

Procedure 2

Cover the bottom of a glass baking dish with egg white and watch to see which areas coagulate first. The egg white is edible, but it's even less tasty than the honey cake.

Procedure 3

Microwave heat-sensitive fax paper for about 7 minutes. There's no way "nuked" fax paper can be a science experiment you can eat, but it does give you a map of your microwave's hot spots.

BOILING MICROWAVED WATER WITHOUT HEAT

In an ordinary oven, heat penetrates food from the outside in. Microwaves can penetrate about an inch

into whatever you're heating. All the water molecules respond wherever they are struck, so if you boil water in a cup with a 2" diameter, the inside molecules are heated at the same time as the outside molecules (except for the hot spots). This accounts for the speed of microwave heating, the main advantage of the oven.

Water boils when the molecules move fast enough to escape from the surface into the air. When you boil water in a pot, the heat source is at the bottom, and the molecules at the bottom move faster than those at the top. In early stages of heating, the molecules lose some of this motion as they encounter cooler molecules on their rise to the top. Boiling is when bubbles of water vapor collect on the bottom of the pot and rise to the surface.

You can create boiling in microwave-heated water by adding some sugar.

Materials & Equipment

◆ 1 cup water
◆ ½ teaspoon sugar
◆ Pyrex measuring cup
◆ measuring spoons

Procedure

1 Fill a Pyrex measuring cup with 1 cup of water and microwave it on high for 2 minutes and 30 seconds.

2 Remove the cup from the oven. Add ½ teaspoon of sugar. See a rush of bubbles come to the surface about a second after you add the sugar.

Observations

When you boil water by microwave, the entire container is evenly heated. Molecules capable of escaping can be right in the middle of the liquid with cooler molecules around the edges, depending on where the hot spots of your oven are located. The sugar crystals act as points of disturbance that bubbles of water vapor form around. The bubbles quickly rise to the surface.

You can also boil water that contains ice. The trick is to put very little water in a Pyrex measuring cup with a lot of ice cubes. Water molecules are free to move when struck by microwaves but frozen water molecules are not. Until the ice is surrounded by enough hot water to liquefy them, they remain solid.

You won't save time trying to microwave frozen soup. In fact, liquid soup can boil away before a solid block of frozen soup melts. Defrosting by microwave consists of alternating a blast of microwaves with a period of no microwaves. The heat picked up by liquid water molecules is transferred to liquefy adjacent frozen molecules during the resting period.

MICROWAVING AWAY STALENESS

As bread ages, it gets stale. The moisture in the bread evaporates, and the bread dries out. Also as time passes, the starch in bread recrystallizes, causing it to become hard or stale. Temperature is one variable that affects staling. Bread will get stale faster at lower temperatures that are above freezing than at room temperature. So putting bread in the refrigerator can hasten its staling, not preserve it. Freezing almost completely stops staling. Can you design an experiment to test this idea?

Stale starch crystals melt at 140°F (60°C). Reheating stale bread seems like a good solution, but even more moisture will be lost, making the bread dryer. But you can freshen stale bread in a microwave: Sprinkle it with water, wrap it in a paper towel, and heat it 5–10 seconds on high.

Microwaving causes water molecules to migrate through food and condense on the surface. This tends to make the surfaces of baked goods gummy instead of crisp. Paper towels wrapped around food absorb some of the surface moisture and keep baked goods from becoming soggy. Microwave ovens destroy a crisp crust. But don't take my word for it; try it and see for yourself. The reason cakes and breads baked in microwaves don't brown is be-

cause water at their surfaces makes them too cool to brown.

You can also freshen bread in a regular oven if you sprinkle it with water, wrap it in foil, and heat it for 3–4 minutes.

MICROWAVE POPCORN

The heating ability of microwaves was discovered accidentally by Dr. Percy Spencer, a researcher on shortwave electromagnetic energy for the Raytheon Company. He was visiting a laboratory that made magnetrons for radar tracking devices. He noticed that the microwaves from a magnetron melted a piece of candy in his pocket. He sent out for a bag of popcorn, which popped when he put it near the magnetron. Although many radar engineers were aware of the heating properties of microwaves, Spencer was the first to apply them to cooking food. Raytheon went on to build the first microwave ovens in 1946. And the rest, as they say, is history.

One of the most successful products designed for the microwave oven is popcorn. The key to microwaved popcorn is not in the corn but in the bag. Do the following experiments to learn more about popcorn and its amazing microwavable bag.

Materials & Equipment

- a package of microwave popcorn
- ½ cup ordinary popping corn
- scissors
- waxed paper
- measuring cup
- 2 large glass bowls
- plastic wrap
- a small, sharp knife
- pot holders

Procedure

1 Cut open the end of a microwave popcorn bag. Empty the contents onto a piece of waxed paper. Notice that the kernels are embedded in a solid, fatty material.

2 Put about ½ cup of embedded kernels in the bottom of a glass bowl. Seal the top with plastic wrap. Make a small slit in the middle of the plastic wrap with a knife.

3 Put the ordinary popping corn in the other glass bowl. Cover this bowl with plastic wrap as well and make a vent.

4 Microwave each bowl of corn separately on high for 4 minutes. Remove the bowls with pot holders. Carefully pull off the plastic wrap. **Warning**: There is a lot of steam trapped in the bowls. Loosen the wrap on the side of the bowl farthest from you and pull it back slowly. This way

your hands and arms will not be exposed to the steam.

Observations

In each sample, see how many unpopped kernels (UPKs) there are. There are about 200 kernels in $\frac{1}{2}$ cup of popcorn, so you can calculate the percentage of UPKs with the following formula:

$$(\text{Number of UPKs} \div 200) \times 100 =$$
$$\text{the percent of UPKs}$$

The solid fatty material that the microwave popcorn comes in converts microwave energy into heat energy and is in direct contact with the kernels. Since the kernels are not agitated as they are in an air popper or when you shake a pot over a flame, the fatty material makes sure that the kernels are all heated fairly evenly. But microwave popcorn still has a higher percentage of UPKs than popcorn popped in oil. (Can you design an experiment to check out this idea?)

The popcorn that is popped dry still pops, but there is usually an even higher percentage of UPKs, and there is also a higher percentage of kernels that are not completely popped.

Food engineers went to work: How could the number of UPKs be reduced? They discovered that the key was not the popcorn but the design of the

bag. For more kernels to pop, you need to concentrate the heat. You are instructed to place the bag in the oven with a particular side down. Cut the bag close to the center panel that is supposed to rest on the oven floor. Tear it toward the center. Notice that the bag is made of three layers. The outer layer is a grease-resistant paper. The inner layer is a grease-proof paper. The middle layer is a polyester

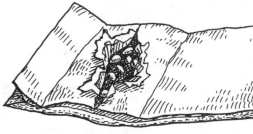

film embedded with a light layer of aluminum. The film absorbs microwaves and becomes hot. An interesting aside: The Stealth bomber is coated with a ceramic embedded with aluminum that absorbs the microwaves of radar and allows the plane to avoid being tracked.

Popcorn also needs space. The problem the engineers faced was how to design a package that could be compact on the supermarket shelf yet be large enough to give the popcorn room to pop. The answer is in the expandable, pleated bag. If the volume of a container is restricted, the popcorn will not pop as large. Can you design an experiment to test this idea?

Microbes

Ever clean out the refrigerator and discover that some once-appetizing foods are now mushy, fuzzy, or foul smelling? Now imagine what our ancestors, who had no refrigerators, had to deal with. Your senses find rotting food unpleasant for good reason: It can make you sick.

Cooking was one way our ancestors tried to delay spoilage. Strong spices and herbs were used to mask the flavor of tainted meat and fish. It is not surprising that the strongest spices, like pepper, chili, and curry, were first used in warm climates, where food spoils more quickly than in colder parts of the world.

But not all the changes in food left to stand were unpleasant. Milk could be made into cheese, grape juice could become wine, flour and water paste developed bubbles and became bread when baked. These pleasant changes became ways of preserving food also. Cheese and wine could be eaten months after they were prepared. Dry grain could be stored without rotting to be ground into flour at some later time. In days where there were no such things as canning, freezing, or refrigerating food, cheese, bread, and wine were a protection against famine. They were among the most important foods of early civilizations.

The change in grape juice as it became wine was so well known that it had its own name, *fermentation*, meaning "to boil." As grape juice ferments, tiny bubbles form that are similar to the bubbles in boiling liquids, except that the grape juice is not hot. Although people have known how to make wine for centuries, it wasn't until the middle of the nineteenth century, when something went wrong with the wine industry of France, that we began to understand what caused grape juice to ferment.

The problem was that some wine went sour as it aged. Since the spoiled wine was prepared in exactly the same way as wine that was good, the wine makers couldn't understand how the spoiling occurred. In desperation, they called in a great scien-

tist, Louis Pasteur (1822–1895), to try to solve their problem.

Pasteur studied the wine in good vats and in spoiled vats. He found that both fermentation and wine spoilage were products of living things, *microbes*, that could be seen only with a microscope. The microbe that fermented grape juice into wine used sugar from the grapes as food and produced alcohol and carbon dioxide as waste products. The microbes that spoiled the wine used alcohol formed by the first microbes as food. It was the wastes of these second microbes that gave the wine a bad taste.

To solve the wine makers' problem Pasteur made the following suggestion: Kill the microbes by heating the wine gently to denature the protein in the microbes but not hot enough to boil the wine. This heating process, called *pasteurization*, is a standard procedure today for killing harmful microbes in dairy products, beer, and wine.

Microbes are everywhere—in air, in water, in soil, in our bodies. The study of microbes has touched on all aspects of human life, including agriculture, medicine, chemical products for industry, and biotechnical engineering as well as food preparation and preservation. The experiments in this chapter will show you how microbes act in some of the foods we eat.

SALLY LUNN BREAD: A STUDY OF YEAST ACTIVITY

Yeasts are one-celled plants that are distant cousins of mushrooms. Like mushrooms and other plants that do not contain chlorophyll, yeasts cannot make their own food and must get it from their surroundings. When conditions are not favorable, yeasts become inactive, only to spring to life when conditions are right.

The products of fermentation, alcohol and carbon dioxide, are of utmost importance to the wine maker and the baker. The wine maker is interested in alcohol production and the baker is interested in carbon dioxide, for it is this gas that makes bread rise.

The next experiment is designed to show what food yeasts need for growth. Other essential conditions for growth—temperature and moisture—will be made as favorable as possible.

Materials & Equipment

- ✦ I package of dry yeast
- ✦ water
- ✦ I tablespoon sugar
- ✦ I tablespoon corn syrup
- ✦ I tablespoon cornstarch

- ✦ measuring cups and spoons
- ✦ a candy thermometer
- ✦ 3 6-ounce glasses
- ✦ 3 spoons
- ✦ a large pot

Procedure

1 Dissolve the yeast in ½ cup of 110°F water. Divide the yeast mixture equally between the 3 glasses.

2 Put 1 tablespoon of sugar in the first glass, 1 tablespoon of corn syrup in the next glass, and 1 tablespoon of cornstarch in the third glass. Stir each glass with a different spoon.

3 Set up a warm-water bath for the yeast in the large pot. Put enough 110°F water in the pot to

come about halfway up the sides of the glasses containing the yeast mixture, as shown in the illustration.

Be sure not to let any of the water from the bath get into the glasses. The bath water will cool slowly, but the temperature will remain warm long enough to generate active fermentation.

Measure fermentation by the size of the bubbles in the foam and the rate at which they form.

Observations

The material a microbe uses as food is called a *substrate*. Which substrate in your experiment starts being fermented first? Which substrate has the steadiest rate of fermentation? Can you smell the alcohol produced by fermentation?

Glucose is the principle food of yeast used for baking. When yeast comes into contact with glucose, fermentation begins immediately. Glucose is present in corn syrup. Yeast can also get glucose from sucrose (table sugar) and starch, but it takes longer to get going, as sucrose and starch have to be broken down into simpler sugars before fermentation can occur. How do your findings support this idea?

Materials & Equipment

✦ ½ cup milk
✦ 1 stick (½ cup) butter

✦ all the mixtures from the preceding experiment

- ✦ about 3½ cups flour
- ✦ I teaspoon salt
- ✦ 3 eggs
- ✦ a medium-sized saucepan
- ✦ a candy thermometer
- ✦ a large bowl
- ✦ an electric mixer
- ✦ a damp, clean dish towel
- ✦ an 8" x 4" x 2" loaf pan
- ✦ a sharp knife
- ✦ a wire rack

Procedure

1 Put the milk and butter in a saucepan and heat until the milk is about 85°F. Don't let the milk get too hot, or you will kill the yeast.

2 Pour all 3 glasses from your experiment into a large bowl and add the milk-and-butter mixture.

3 Add about a cup of the flour and the salt to the liquids. Mix at low speed with an electric mixer. When all the flour is moistened, beat the batter for about 2 minutes at a medium speed to develop the gluten.

4 Beat in the eggs and add another cup of flour. Finally add enough of the remaining flour to make a stiff batter that can still be stirred.

5 Cover the bowl with a moist, clean dish towel and place in a warm spot to rise.

While the batter is rising, grease the loaf pan and sprinkle a few tablespoons of flour on the pan.

Shake it so that the flour evenly coats all sides of the pan, and dump out any extra flour.

6 Let the batter rise until it doubles in size— about an hour. Then punch it down with your fist. What gives the batter its stretchy consistency? Examine the air pockets in the batter. Are they evenly distributed? Are there larger air pockets near the source of heat?

7 Beat the batter for about 30 seconds. Put the batter in the loaf pan, cover with the dish towel, and let it rise again until it has doubled in size (about an hour). Preheat the oven to 325°F.

8 Bake the bread at 325°F for about 50 minutes. It is done when the sides draw slightly away from the sides of the pan. Run a sharp knife around the bread as soon as you take it from the oven. Remove the bread from the pan and let it cool on a wire rack. Sally Lunn bread is best served while still warm.

PRETZELS:
INHIBITING YEAST ACTION

When you add other chemicals to the yeast environment, you can affect fermentation. The next experiment shows how.

Materials & Equipment

+ 1 package of dry yeast
+ water
+ ½ teaspoon sugar
+ ¼ teaspoon salt
+ a candy thermometer

+ measuring cups and spoons
+ 3 small glasses
+ 3 spoons
+ a large pot

Procedure

1 Dissolve the yeast in 1 cup of 110°F water. Divide the yeast solution between the 3 glasses.

2 Put ¼ teaspoon sugar in the first glass and ¼ teaspoon salt plus ¼ teaspoon sugar in the second glass. Leave the third glass untreated as a control. Stir each glass with a different spoon.

3 Make a warm-water bath as you did for the previous experiment. Put the 3 glasses in the water bath and watch for fermentation activity.

Observations

Which glass has the most activity? Which glass has the least? Does salt inhibit yeast activity? How can you tell?

Use this experiment to make pretzels.

Materials & Equipment

- yeast mixtures from your experiment
- about 4½ cups flour
- vegetable oil
- 1 egg yolk, beaten
- 1 tablespoon water
- coarse (kosher) salt
- 2 large bowls
- a big spoon
- a clean, damp dish towel
- a cookie sheet
- a small bowl
- a whisk or fork
- a pastry brush

Procedure

1 Pour the contents of your experiment into a large bowl. Add between 4 and 4½ cups flour. Mix to form a stiff dough.

2 Knead the dough on a floured surface for about 8 minutes. Kneading develops the gluten, which is the only protein that supports pretzels. (Sally Lunn bread has milk and eggs to help do this job.) To knead, turn the dough out onto a floured surface and rub some flour on your hands to keep them from sticking to the dough. Fold over, toward you, the side of the

dough farthest from you. Push the fold into the rest of the dough with the heel of your hand. Give the dough a quarter turn and repeat the motion. Dough that has been properly kneaded is no longer sticky but smooth and elastic.

3 Oil a large bowl and put in the kneaded dough, turning it so the surface becomes slightly oiled and will not dry out. Cover the dough with a clean, damp towel. Let it rise in a warm place until it doubles in size.

4 While the dough is rising, grease the cookie sheet and make the egg mixture: Separate an egg. In a small bowl or custard cup beat the yolk together with 1 tablespoon of water using a whisk or a fork.

5 When the dough is finished rising, punch it down with your fist. Break off balls of dough and roll them between your hands into long ropes. Then shape them into pretzels and put them on the cookie sheet. You can make many different shapes.

6 Use a pastry brush to paint each pretzel with the egg yolk mixture. Sprinkle the pretzels with coarse salt.

7 Preheat the oven to 475°F. Let the pretzels rise again in a warm place until they have almost doubled in size. Then bake them for about 10 minutes or until the pretzels are firm and golden brown.

A COMPARISON OF YOGURT CULTURES

Bacteria are one-celled microbes that are smaller than yeast. Bacteria, like yeast, must also get food from their surroundings, and they can use many substances as food. Some even live on such unappetizing materials as rubber and petroleum. The bacteria you'll be experimenting with live on milk.

Milk is a mixture of many substances—water, proteins, fats, and a sugar, found only in milk, known as *lactose*. Certain bacteria feed on lactose and give off *lactic acid* as a waste product.

As lactic-acid bacteria grow, more and more lactic acid collects, giving the milk a sour taste, typical of acids. What is even more striking than the change in taste is the change in texture. Lactic acid causes milk proteins to become denatured, making the milk thicker and thicker. Such cultured milk, called yogurt, has a nutty, sour taste and a custardy texture.

Frozen yogurt has become a popular dessert. But the first frozen yogurts were simply frozen versions of traditional yogurt, and they did not sell. People did not like sour ice cream. The successful versions on the market today use different strains of bacteria in the culture. Culture your own yogurt at home using two different starter cultures to see what the difference really is.

It is simple to make yogurt at home. The recipe that follows is certain to produce good results because you will be creating ideal conditions for the growth of lactic-acid bacteria.

Materials & Equipment

+ $\frac{1}{2}$ gallon skim milk
+ $\frac{1}{2}$ cup of commercially prepared plain yogurt
+ I cup melted vanilla frozen yogurt
+ a saucepan
+ a candy thermometer
+ measuring cups
+ 2 medium-sized bowls
+ 2 spoons
+ 2 clean I$\frac{1}{2}$-quart glass jars with covers
+ labels
+ a pen
+ 2 dish towels
+ I insulated picnic cooler

Procedure

1 Warm the milk in the pan over low heat until a skin forms (160°F). This kills any bacteria that may cause the milk to spoil before the yogurt forms. Let the milk cool until it is 110°F.

2 Mix ½ cup of yogurt and 1 cup of the warm milk in a bowl. Next, mix 1 cup of melted frozen yogurt with 1 cup of warm milk in another bowl. Divide the remaining warm milk equally between the 2 glass jars.

3 Stir each of the starter cultures into a different jar of milk. Label the jars so you know which contains the plain yogurt starter culture and which contains the frozen yogurt starter culture.

4 Wrap each jar in a dish towel and place in the cooler. Cover the cooler and check your yogurt after about 6 hours. The yogurt is finished when it moves away from the side of the container in one piece if you tilt it. Refrigerate the finished yogurt to stop the growth of the bacteria.

Observations

Which culture finished first? Which was more sour? How does the consistency compare? Look at the labels on the original containers of both yogurts. Which type has more ingredients? The plain yogurt uses a strain of bacteria called *Lactobacillus acidophilus*. Frozen yogurts don't usually identify the microbes they use, but it is normally a combination of *Streptococcus thermophilus* and *Lactobacillus bulgaricus* in secret proportions.

The recipe produced good results because you created ideal conditions for the growth of lactic-acid bacteria. Try making yogurt at different temperatures. Compare yogurt made with fresh whole milk, condensed milk, and powdered milk. Find out what happens when you add sugar to the milk. Use different brands of commercially prepared yogurt as starter cultures. Try using acidophilus powders or capsules from a health food store as starter cultures. See how many generations of yogurt you can produce from the yogurt you make. Use red-cabbage indicator to measure changes in acidity as the culture grows.

Your yogurt may be eaten plain or mixed with fresh fruit, fruit preserves, honey, maple syrup, or a small amount of defrosted concentrated orange juice.

Enzymes

In 1897 Eduard Buechner, a German chemist, ground up some yeast cells and made an extract from them. He put this extract in grape juice and found, to his astonishment, that the grape juice still fermented. For the first time, glucose became alcohol and carbon dioxide without using living cells. The substance in Buechner's extract that caused fermentation was called *enzyme*, from the Greek roots *en* and *zyme* meaning "leavened."

Today we think of enzymes as the molecules that control the countless numbers of chemical reactions in living organisms. The role of enzymes becomes impressive when you take a close look at a

few of the reactions that take place in a living thing. The oxidation of food, for example, does not burn in your body the way it burns in a calorimeter. If it did, a piece of chocolate cake containing 400 calories would raise the body temperature of a 100-pound person to about 117°F, high enough to cause death. In your body, food combines with many different substances in a chain of reactions in which a little energy is released with each step. Controlled release of energy during the oxidation of food allows this energy to be used for the work that the body does in all its activities, including movement, digestion, repair of injured tissues, sensing the environment, and so on. Without enzymes, life is not possible.

RENNET CUSTARD:
A STUDY OF ENZYME ACTION

One of the first steps in the digestion of milk is denaturing milk protein, or curdling it, so it becomes more solid. If milk remained a liquid, it would quickly pass through the stomach before it could be digested. But curdled milk moves slowly enough for digestion to take place.

A great many things will denature milk protein,

including heat and acids. In the stomachs of mammals, milk protein is denatured by an enzyme called *rennin* (or, commercially, *rennet*).

Rennet used to be prepared commercially from the linings of calves' stomachs. But today you can buy vegetable-based rennet tablets in some health food stores. They are used for preparing cottage cheese and thickening milk desserts. The next experiment will show you some of the properties of enzymes by varying the conditions necessary for the enzyme to work.

Materials & Equipment

- ✦ 3 teaspoons water
- ✦ vegetable-based liquid rennet
- ✦ 1½ cups whole milk
- ✦ 6 teaspoons sugar
- ✦ vanilla
- ✦ measuring cups and spoons
- ✦ 3 6-ounce clear custard cups
- ✦ masking tape
- ✦ a pen or marker
- ✦ a spoon
- ✦ a saucepan
- ✦ a candy thermometer

Procedure

1 Put 1 teaspoon of water in each of the 3 cups. Add a drop of rennet to each and swirl to mix. Label each cup, using masking tape. They should read: "cold," "110°F," and "160°F."

2 Put $\frac{1}{2}$ cup cold milk in a measuring cup. Add 2 teaspoons sugar and a dash (less than $\frac{1}{4}$ teaspoon) of vanilla and stir well. Pour the mixture into the cup labeled "cold" and stir well.

3 Mix another $\frac{1}{2}$ cup of milk with sugar and vanilla. Warm this in a saucepan until its temperature is 110°F. Pour into the cup labeled "110°F" and stir well.

4 Make another milk mixture and heat this one to 160°F. Pour into the remaining cup and stir well. Let the mixtures stand, without disturbing them, until they set (if they do).

Observations

In which cup does the custard become firm most quickly? In which does it fail to set? How does this support the idea that enzymes are proteins? (Hint: What happens to proteins when they are heated to a high temperature?) What does this tell you about the amount of an enzyme needed to cause a reaction? Try the experiment with two drops of rennet and see if it makes a difference.

Do an experiment to see if rennet will work on other proteins. Substitute soybean milk, skim milk, non-fat dry milk, or evaporated milk. Suppose you denature the milk some other way, like boiling it. Let the boiled milk cool to 110°F before adding it

to the rennet. How do your findings support the idea that rennin, like many other enzymes, controls only one reaction—in this case, denaturing milk protein?

CUT APPLES: KIWI STOPS THE BROWNING

The browning-of-fruit reaction studied in Vitamin C Fruit Salad (see Chapter 6, pages 121–25) is more complicated than simple oxidation. An enzyme called *polyphenol oxidase* is involved. This enzyme causes certain compounds in cells to react with oxygen and become brown or gray. The reaction is similar to human skin turning brown in the sun. When the cells are intact, the enzyme and the compounds in the tissues (the phenols) are not in contact. When you cut an apple, the enzyme is released to act on the phenols and the browning reaction starts.

Is there any way to stop or slow down enzymatic browning? Do the next experiment and find out.

Materials & Equipment

- ✦ a kiwifruit
- ✦ an apple
- ✦ a knife
- ✦ a new sponge
- ✦ scissors

Procedure

1 Peel the brown skin off the kiwi and slice the fruit.

2 Cut out a piece of sponge about the same size as a slice of kiwi.

3 Cut the apple in half. Place a slice of kiwi on the cut surface of one half of the apple. Place the piece of sponge on the cut surface of the other half of the apple. Wait at least 1 hour, or until the exposed surface of the apple is brown. Lift the sponge and the piece of kiwi.

Observations

What color is the apple under the kiwi and under the sponge? The sponge was the control so that you could see what happens when the surface is shielded from the air. Is shielding from air sufficient to slow down the browning reaction? There obviously is some substance in the kiwi that interferes with the browning reaction. In lemons that substance is vitamin C, also called ascorbic acid. Kiwis are another source of this compound. You might

want to compare how kiwis, lemons, and a solution of vitamin C slow down enzymatic browning in apples. Design an experiment to do this.

JELL-O WITH PINEAPPLE: HOW HEAT AFFECTS AN ENZYME

If you read the instructions on a box of Jell-O, you are warned never to add fresh or frozen pineapple to the dessert. This warning is a perfect opening for a science experiment. Fresh pineapple contains an enzyme called bromelain that breaks down proteins. Gelatin desserts are protein, and the bromelain in fresh pineapple would break down the protein so the dessert wouldn't gel. Since the enzymes themselves are also protein, it makes sense that heat can denature the enzyme and make it inactive. Do the next experiment to see the effect of heat on enzyme action.

Materials & Equipment

- ✦ a fresh, ripe pineapple
- ✦ a package of Jell-O
- ✦ water
- ✦ a large, sharp knife
- ✦ 6 clear plastic cups
- ✦ a marker
- ✦ a plate
- ✦ a small saucepan
- ✦ a bowl
- ✦ measuring cups and spoons

Procedure

1 Since pineapples are difficult to cut, get an adult to help you. Cut the pineapple into quarters. Taking one quarter, cut away the rind and the hard, inner core. Then cut the fruit into bite-sized pieces. Make them all the same size.

2 You are going to heat the pieces of pineapple different lengths of time in the microwave. Raw pineapple will be the control. So mark one of the plastic cups "raw" and put 2 pieces of fresh pineapple into that cup. Mark the rest of the cups as follows: "10 seconds," "30 seconds," "1 minute," "2 minutes," and "boiled."

3 Put 8 pieces of pineapple on a plate in the microwave oven. Microwave on high for 10 seconds. Quickly remove 2 pieces and put them in the cup marked "10 seconds." Immediately microwave the remaining pineapple on high for 20 seconds. Remove 2 pieces and put them in the cup marked "30 seconds." Microwave the remaining pineapple for 30 seconds and then remove 2 pieces and put them in the cup marked "1 minute." Microwave the last 2 pieces for another minute. Remove them and put them in the cup marked "2 minutes."

4 Next put 2 pieces of pineapple in a small saucepan. Cover with water and boil them for 5 minutes. Drain off the water, and place these

pieces in the last cup, marked "boiled."

5 Mix the Jell-O according to the directions on the package. Spoon 4 tablespoons of liquid Jell-O into each cup, then put them in the refrigerator to cool.

Observations

Which cups gelled? Do your findings support the idea that a high temperature alone is not enough to "kill" an enzyme? Is the length of time the enzyme is exposed to a high heat also a factor?

Other fruits also contain protein-splitting enzymes. Design an experiment using Jell-O to see which fruits they are.

BAKED STEAK: ACIDS, BASES, AND ENZYME ACTION

Papain is an enzyme that is commercially prepared from papayas, a tropical fruit. It is one of a number of enzymes found in plants and animals that break down proteins. For this reason, papain is sold as a meat tenderizer.

The purpose of the next experiment is to answer two questions: Is meat treated with papain

more tender than untreated meat? Does an acid or a base have an effect on the tenderizing activity of papain?

Of course, to answer these questions we have to have a way of measuring meat tenderness. Here's where science gets creative. I tried cutting the meat with a knife and piercing it with a fork and estimating the force I needed. But this kind of measurement is very subjective and inaccurate. So I finally came up with feeding my experiment to an unsuspecting friend, one piece of meat at a time, and counting the number of chews before swallowing. The tenderer the meat, the fewer the chews.

Needless to say, counting chews is not the most precise method of measuring tenderness. Two pieces of meat, prepared in exactly the same manner, might require different numbers of chews depending on the size of the pieces, whether or not there was gristle, how it tasted, how dry the chewer's mouth was, whether or not the chewer expected it to be tender, and how hungry the chewer was.

Since there are so many known possibilities of error, the procedure for this experiment is the most elaborate one in this book. You will be taking precautions wherever possible to reduce the sources of error.

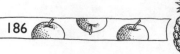

Materials & Equipment

- ✦ ¾ pound round steak. (When you buy the steak, look for the most evenly red piece with very little fat and gristle and a uniform thickness.)
- ✦ water
- ✦ ¾ teaspoon unseasoned meat tenderizer
- ✦ vinegar
- ✦ baking soda
- ✦ a sharp knife
- ✦ a cutting board
- ✦ a fork
- ✦ 6 bowls
- ✦ index cards
- ✦ pencil and paper
- ✦ 5 juice glasses
- ✦ measuring spoons
- ✦ 5 spoons
- ✦ scissors
- ✦ a broiling pan
- ✦ 6 plates
- ✦ a pot with a cover
- ✦ barrier for table
- ✦ A hungry friend who doesn't know anything about your experiment. Tell your friend you will call when you are ready.

Procedure

Trim any fat and gristle from the meat and cut the trimmed meat into ¾-inch cubes. Try to keep the size of the cubes as uniform as possible. Pierce each piece of meat twice with a fork. (This is to allow the solutions you will be putting on the

meat to penetrate inside.) Mix up all the cubes of meat in a pile.

2 Set the 6 bowls in a row. Deal out the cubes of meat, as you would deal cards, into the 6 bowls to form 6 equal groups of meat cubes. Try and get the same number in each group. If you have any extra pieces, put them in the last (control) group. Set an index card above each bowl and number the groups 1 through 6.

3 Put juice glasses in front of groups 1 through 5 and put 2 tablespoons of water in each glass. Put 2 tablespoons of water on the meat in group 6.

Put ¼ teaspoon of meat tenderizer in the glasses in front of groups 1, 2, and 3.

¼ Teaspoon
Meat Tenderizer

¼ Teaspoon
Meat Tenderizer
½ Teaspoon
Vinegar

¼ Teaspoon
Meat Tenderizer
½ Teaspoon
Baking Soda

½ Teaspoon
Vinegar

½ Teaspoon
Baking Soda

2 TABLESPOONS
Water

Put ½ teaspoon of vinegar in the solutions for groups 2 and 4.

Put ½ teaspoon baking soda in the glasses for groups 3 and 5.

So, the solutions you've created for each group are:

Group 1: Meat tenderizer and water

Group 2: Meat tenderizer, acid, water

Group 3: Meat tenderizer, base, water

Group 4: Acid, water

Group 5: Base, water

Group 6: Water

Stir each solution with a different spoon and pour over its group of meat cubes. Be sure to thoroughly moisten all the meat in each group.

4 Preheat the oven to 400°F. Let the meat stand in the solutions while the oven is preheating and you complete the next step.

5 The order in which each piece of meat is chewed can affect your results. The best way to reduce this source of error is to present the pieces of meat in a completely random order. Here's one way to come up with a random list of numbers:

a. Cut index cards into as many small squares as the *total number* of pieces of meat in your experiment. If you have 6 groups of 10 pieces each, you will need 60 small squares.

b Put the numeral "1" on as many squares of card as you have pieces of meat in group 1. If you have 10 pieces, 10 squares of index card should be marked "1." Do the same for groups 2, 3, 4, 5, and 6.

c Put all the numbered squares in a bowl. Cover the bowl and shake it to mix up all the squares. Draw out one square at a time, without looking, and mark down the number on a piece of paper. The order might look something like this:

4, 4, 6, 6, 6, 2, 1, 1, 3, 5, 6, 4, etc.

6 After you have made out your table of random numbers, drain the solutions from each bowl and put the drained meat on the broiling pan in separate groups. Keep the groups in the right order so you know which is which. Arrange the meat in a single layer with the pieces spaced fairly evenly so

all the pieces will be heated the same amount. Bake for 15 minutes.

7 While the meat is baking, prepare a sheet of paper to record your data:

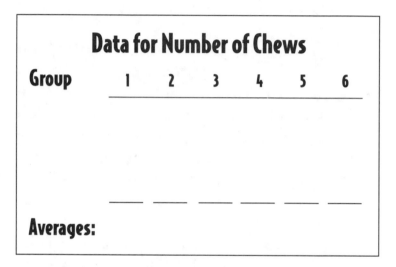

Data for Number of Chews

Group	1	2	3	4	5	6

Averages:

Test the meat for doneness by pressing with a fork. It should be springy and firm. Meat that is rare will be softer, as all the protein has not been set by heat.

8 Put each group of cubes on a plate and label it using your numbered index cards again. Set up a table with some kind of barrier so your friend cannot see where each piece comes from. Get your data sheet and pencil, your table of random numbers and call your friend.

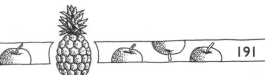

9 Show your friend where to sit. Say: "I'm going to give you pieces of baked steak to eat. I am testing the meat for tenderness. Please count the number of chews you need for each piece before you swallow it. Chew as naturally as possible."

Your table of random numbers tells you the order of choosing pieces of meat. If the first three numerals were 4, 4, 6, you would give your friend a piece from Group 4, another piece from Group 4, and a piece from Group 6, in that order. Check off each number on your table as your friend chews the meat.

Record the number of chews for each piece in the proper column on your data sheet. When you have the data for all the pieces of meat, take the average for each group.

Observations

Was meat treated with tenderizer more tender than untreated meat? (Compare the averages for Group 1 and Group 6.) Did acid or base alone affect meat tenderness? (Compare Groups 4 and 5 with Group 6.) Did acid have an effect on the action of the enzyme? (Compare Groups 1 and 2.) Did a base have an effect on enzyme action? (Compare Groups 1 and 3.)

If you are not certain of your results, compare

them with the data on the next page that I obtained when I did the experiment. Your numbers may be very different, but you probably will come to the same conclusions.

You can use the procedure for this experiment to test many other substances. See if you get similar results with another acid, such as vitamin C. Try the experiment on other kinds of meat. Find out if the enzyme has any other effect on meat, like juiciness. Can you think of a way to modify the procedure so that you can measure juiciness? You might find using another kind of meat, like hamburger, useful for studying the enzyme's effect on juiciness. You might also do an experiment to see if you can denature the enzyme by heating it. Boil an enzyme solution before you put it on the meat and compare its activity with an unheated enzyme in solution.

Data for Number of Chews

Group	1	2	3	4	5	6
	26	42	25	54	44	45
	35	33	28	53	22	29
	29	25	20	48	27	54
	32	35	18	30	47	37
						60
Averages:	30.5	33.75	22.75	46.25	35.0	45.0

Cooking Terms and Instructions

basting: To moisten food while it cooks, so that the surface doesn't dry out and flavor is added, coat it with its own juices or a prepared marinade. A pastry brush is helpful, but you can also use a spoon.

beating egg whites: Start with egg whites that are at room temperature. It is best to use an electric mixer for beating egg whites. (If you don't have one, use an egg beater or a wire whisk. You might want to have a friend handy to help when your arm gets tired.) Beat the whites on low speed until they become foamy, then increase the speed gradually to high and beat until the whites become stiff. They should have a glossy surface and will stand in peaks when you lift the beater slowly from the bowl. Don't

overbeat egg whites or they will start to dry out.

boiling: When a liquid
 boils, bubbles are
 constantly rising to the
 surface and breaking.

creaming: Creaming
 is used to mix a
 shortening like butter
with other ingredients such as sugar until well
blended. It is easiest to cream butter with an electric
mixer, and the mixture will be fluffier and lighter in
color if you do. If you don't have an electric mixer,
you can do it by hand with a large spoon (a wooden
spoon works well) and a lot of muscle. Either way
you should start with softened butter. To cream by
hand, press down on the butter with the back of the
spoon, drawing the spoon towards you across the
bottom of the bowl. Turn the bowl as you go and pe-
riodically scrape around the sides of the bowl to collect the ingredients in the middle again. Continue
creaming until the mixture is thoroughly combined
and smooth.

cutting in: Cutting in is done to distribute solid fat in
 flour by using a pastry blender or two knives until
 flour-coated fat particles are the size you want. If
 you have a pastry blender, roll the blades along the
 bottom of the bowl, then lift it up, turn the bowl and

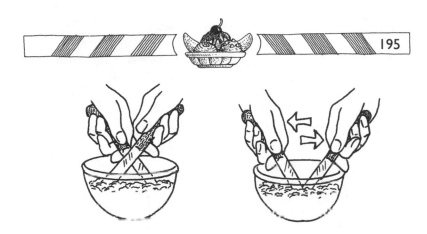

slice down again. You'll need to stop and scrape off the blender and bring all the ingredients into the center every few turns. If you're using two knives, take a knife in each hand. Start with your hands close together over the center of the bowl then move them apart, drawing the two blades across each other, scraping the bottom of the bowl as you go.

dropping by spoonfuls: Take a spoonful of batter for cookies or biscuits and push it off onto your baking sheet with another spoon or your fingers. Leave a couple of inches between drops to give them room to spread out as they bake.

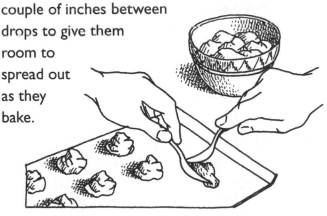

folding: Folding is a way to combine delicate ingredients such as whipped cream or beaten egg whites with other foods without losing too much of the volume and the air bubbles. Add the whipped ingredient to the heavier ingredient and, using a rubber spatula, cut down into the mixture, slide across the bottom of the bowl, and bring some of the mixture up and over the surface. Give the bowl a quarter turn and repeat this circular motion. Continue to fold just until the two ingredients are combined. If you fold too much, you'll lose more air than necessary, and your cake won't rise as high.

kneading dough: Flour your hands liberally, then turn the dough out onto a lightly floured surface and shape it into a ball. Pull the far end of the dough toward you, folding it over. Then, using the heels of your hands, push it away with a rolling motion. Give the dough a quarter turn and continue folding and pushing the dough, adding flour as necessary to keep the dough from sticking. Get yourself into a rhythm

and use your whole body, not just your arms, when you knead. You'll need to knead for about ten minutes to make the dough smooth and elastic.

measuring dry ingredients: Scoop up dry ingredients in your measuring cup, or spoon them lightly into the cup. Level off with a knife or other straight edge. Use this scoop-and-sweep method with your measuring spoons as well.

measuring liquids: Use a glass measuring cup with a spout for measuring liquids. Pour the liquid into the cup and check the measure at eye level. Liquids measured in measuring spoons should fill the spoon but not overflow.

preparing baking pans: For cakes, muffins, and cupcakes: Rub the inner surface of a baking dish with butter or vegetable fat. Then add a tablespoon or so of flour and swirl it around in the pan to coat all the surfaces. Dump out any extra flour. For breads, cookies, or biscuits: Just grease the inside of the pan or the surface of the baking sheet. This should ensure that your cakes, breads, and cookies will not stick to the pan.

separating eggs: Have two bowls ready, one for the white and one for the yolk. Gently crack the egg

1.

2.

3.

4.

5.

close to the middle against the edge of a bowl, or by tapping it with a knife. Carefully pull apart the shell with your thumbs and finger- tips. Tip one half of the shell to catch the yolk and let the egg white slip into a bowl. Pass the egg yolk from shell to shell until all the white has run into the bowl, then drop the egg yolk into a second bowl. Don't let any egg yolk mix with the whites. For egg whites to be beaten to their absolute peaks, they cannot be mixed with any fat. If you are separating several eggs, it is safer to let each white drop into a new bowl; that way if the yolk of one egg breaks, it won't ruin the whole bowl of whites.

simmering: A simmering liquid is below the boiling point. Bubbles form slowly and collapse just below the surface.

whipping cream: You can whip cream with an electric mixer, an eggbeater, or a wire whisk. Cream whips faster when cold, so if you are beating cream by hand, it might help to place the bowl of cream over a bowl of ice cubes. Beat the cream at high speed until soft peaks form when you raise the beater straight up.

Equivalent Measures

pinch = less than $\frac{1}{4}$ teaspoon

dash = 2 or 3 drops

1 tablespoon = 3 teaspoons = $\frac{1}{2}$ ounce

1 ounce = 2 tablespoons

1 cup = 16 tablespoons = 8 ounces = $\frac{1}{2}$ pint (liquid)

1 pint = 2 cups = 16 ounces (liquid)

1 quart = 2 pints = 4 cups = 32 ounces

1 gallon = 4 quarts = 8 pints = 16 cups = 128 ounces

1 pound = 16 ounces

1 cup broth = 1 bouillon cube dissolved in 1 cup water

1 quarter-pound stick of butter = $\frac{1}{2}$ cup = 8 tablespoons

1 envelope of gelatin = 1 tablespoon

Science Glossary

acid: Any substance that can react with a base to form a salt. In water solutions an acid tastes sour, as in lemon juice or vinegar, but tasting is not a good method for testing for acids since many acids are dangerous. Sulfuric acid and nitric acid can burn the skin and eat away at metals. Citric acid in oranges and acetic acid in vinegar are harmless, and ascorbic acid (vitamin C) is needed by the body.

alchemist: A chemist who lived during the Middle Ages whose aim was to change other metals into gold.

alkali: Any soluble substance that can neutralize acids to form salts. Also called a base.

amino acids: Molecules made up of carbon, hydro-

gen, oxygen, nitrogen, and sometimes sulfur that link together into chains to form proteins. When protein is digested, it is broken down into its amino acids, and then the amino acids reconnect to make up the kind of protein needed by the digester.

atom: The smallest particle of an element that still has the chemical properties of that element. Atoms of one element can combine with atoms of one or more other elements to produce compounds.

bacteria: Microscopic one-celled organisms that have no chlorophyll. Bacteria are found almost everywhere on earth, including in and on the human body. Some bacteria are harmful and cause diseases, but others are beneficial, such as the bacteria that turn milk into cheese.

base: Any compound that can react with an acid to neutralize it and form a salt. Base solutions are bitter and can also conduct electricity. Baking soda when dissolved in water is a base. Also called alkali.

bromelain: An enzyme found in fresh pineapple that breaks down proteins.

buffer: A substance that can absorb acid or basic molecules and take them out of solution.

carbohydrate: A substance made up of carbon, hydrogen, and oxygen with two hydrogen atoms and one oxygen atom for every atom of carbon. Sugar and starch are both carbohydrates.

cell: The smallest unit of a living thing. Cells are made up of a substance called protoplasm surrounded by a thin membrane.

cell membrane: The outer skin of a cell.

cellulose: A carbohydrate contained in the cell walls of plants that helps to support their structure.

chemical reaction: Any change that alters the chemical properties of a substance, or that forms a new substance.

chlorophyll: The green pigment in plants that gives them the ability to make food for themselves through photosynthesis.

cholesterol: A white, waxy substance found in animal fat, blood, and nerve tissue. If too much cholesterol is present in the blood vessels that nourish your heart, it can cause heart disease.

clarify: To make clear or free from impurities.

coagulation: The process by which a liquid becomes a soft semisolid. Coagulation is one way a protein is denatured.

coalesce: To grow together; to merge.

collagen: A solid protein that will not dissolve in water. Collagen is found in cartilage, tendons, ligaments, and bones.

colloid: A homogeneous mixture made up of two phases, the solvent and the solute, in which the particles of the solute are larger than single molecules

but are small enough to remain suspended in the mixture permanently. A colloid is between a solution and a suspension.

compound: A pure substance made up of fixed amounts of two or more different elements. A compound differs from a mixture because the substances forming the compound lose their individual characteristics, and the compound takes on its own, often quite different, characteristics.

continuous: Going on or extending without a break. Describes the solvent phase of a solution or suspension, in which all the particles of the solvent are in contact with each other.

control: The part of an experiment that is used to check or compare results.

crystal: A solid bit of pure matter in which the atoms or molecules are arranged in a definite pattern so that the solid has a regular geometric shape with many sides or faces. Examples are salt and sugar.

decant: To pour off gently, leaving the sediment behind. Decanting is one method used to separate two parts of a suspension.

denature: To change the nature of a protein by adding heat, acid, base, etc., so that the original properties are greatly changed or eliminated.

density: A measure of the mass of an object in proportion to its volume. For example, a block of lead

will weigh much more than an equal-sized block of wood. That means that lead is denser than wood.

diffusion: An intermingling of the molecules of liquids or gases. The process by which solute particles move through a solvent to form a solution.

discontinuous: Broken up by interruptions or gaps. Describes the solute phase of a solution or suspension in which the particles are not in contact with each other, but are separated by the solvent.

electromagnetic radiation: Waves of energy that radiate through space, including light waves, radio waves, X rays, and microwaves.

element: The simplest form of pure matter. There are ninety-two naturally occuring elements on the earth and eleven man-made elements.

emulsifying agent: A substance that will keep two immiscible liquids from separating, creating an emulsion.

emulsion: A suspension of two immiscible liquids that does not separate on standing.

enzyme: A complex protein found in living things that controls chemical reactions without being changed itself.

fermentation: A chemical change in sugars brought about by the enzymes of living organisms such as yeast. The transformation of grape juice to wine is a good example.

flocculation: The process of drawing impurities out of a substance by collecting them in bunches.

fructose: A simple sugar found in fruits.

gelatin: A jellylike, soluble protein derived from collagen by heating it with water. When gelatin cools, it forms a clear solid.

gelatinization: The process by which a substance swells when it is heated with water.

glucose: A simple sugar found in fruits, green plants, and blood.

gluten: A mixture of proteins found in wheat and other grains. Gluten gives dough a tough, elastic quality.

homogeneous: Composed of similar or identical parts. In the study of fluids, describes a solution or a colloid in which the solute is evenly mixed into the solvent.

hygroscopic: Describes a substance that absorbs moisture from the air.

immiscible: Describes a liquid that cannot be mixed or blended with another liquid. An immiscible liquid will not form a solution.

indicator: A substance that changes its color or some other property when combined with a solution in which an acid or base is present. For example, litmus paper is an indicator that turns blue when dipped in a base, and pink when dipped in acid.

lactic acid: A waste product of bacteria that feed off lactose.

lactose: A simple sugar found in milk.

magnetron: A device that uses a magnet to make electrons move rapidly in a circular path. Found in microwave ovens.

matter: Anything that has weight and takes up space. Matter can usually be classified as a solid, a liquid, or a gas and is made up of atoms.

microbe: A microscopic living thing such as a bacterium. Microbes are often associated with disease or with fermentation.

microwave: A type of energy that causes the water molecules in a substance to move.

molecule: The smallest particle of a substance that can exist and still retain the characteristics of the substance. The molecule of an element consists of one atom or two or more similar atoms, while the molecule of a compound consists of two or more different atoms.

optically active: Describes a substance that has the ability to rotate polarized light.

optics: The science of the nature and properties of light and vision.

osmosis: The movement of molecules of a solvent through a membrane that separates two solutions. The process by which water is absorbed into roots.

oxidation: The chemical reaction of a substance with oxygen.

pasteurization: A method of killing harmful microbes in dairy products, wine, and beer by heating them to denature the protein in the microbes.

photosynthesis: The process by which green plants make sugar from water and air in the presence of chlorophyll, using light energy.

pigment: A natural substance that gives color to the tissues of plants or animals.

polarized light: Light with light rays all vibrating in the same direction. Normal light contains rays vibrating in all directions.

polarizer: A lens, say of a pair of sunglasses, that filters light so that when ordinary light passes through, only light that is traveling in a single direction emerges from the lens.

precipitate: Solid particles that form in a liquid.

protein: A complex compound made up of amino acids. Proteins are found in all animal or plant matter and are essential to the diet of animals.

protoplasm: The living material of all cells.

puree: A suspension of food particles in a liquid: for example, pea soup or tomato sauce.

rennin: An enzyme, found in the stomachs of mammals, which will denature milk protein. This enzyme is commercially distributed under the name **rennet**.

saturated solution: A solution that has absorbed as much of a solute as possible at a given temperature.

serial dilution: A systematic way of varying the amount of water in a solution.

simple sugar: A sugar that contains only 5 or 6 carbon atoms per molecule.

sol: The liquid stage of a colloid, such as gelatin, dissolved in water. When cooled, it sets into the gel form.

solute: The discontinuous phase of a solution.

solution: A homogeneous mixture with two phases, the solvent and the solute, in which the particles of the solute are the size of single molecules and disperse into the solvent permanently so that the mixture remains homogeneous or evenly mixed.

solvent: A substance that dissolves another substance. The continuous phase of a solution.

starch: A complex carbohydrate found in potatoes, rice, corn, wheat, and other food. A starch molecule is made of long chains of simple sugar molecules.

substrate: The material a microbe uses for food.

sucrose: Table sugar. Sucrose is a two-molecule chain with one molecule of glucose and one molecule of fructose.

supersaturated solution: A clear solution that contains more solute than would normally dissolve at a certain temperature.

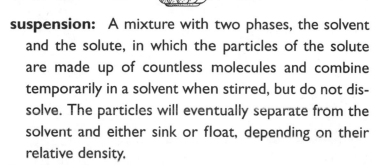

suspension: A mixture with two phases, the solvent and the solute, in which the particles of the solute are made up of countless molecules and combine temporarily in a solvent when stirred, but do not dissolve. The particles will eventually separate from the solvent and either sink or float, depending on their relative density.

Tyndall effect: A phenomenon in which particles of a certain size reflect light. You can see the Tyndall effect in a beam of sunlight in a dusty room. Dust particles are big enough to reflect light, while air molecules are too small.

xylem: A stiff, long strand found in plants such as celery, that carries water from the roots of the plant to the leaves.

Index

Page numbers in *italics* refer to illustrations.